Tallahassee Writers Association

SEVEN HILLS REVIEW
2021

Tallahassee Writers Association

SEVEN HILLS REVIEW
2021

Volume 26

turtle cove press

Tallahassee, Florida

ISBN: 978-1-947536-06-7

Managing Editor: M.R. Street, MPH, MSI
Copy Editor: Lisa Blackwell, Draft Works
Cover Photo: Bruce Ballister, 2020

Other titles published by Turtle Cove Press are available at
https://www.turtlecovepress.com.

Dedicated to
Bruce Ballister

This edition of The Seven Hills Review is dedicated to Bruce Ballister, a superhero in our eyes. Bruce ran the Seven Hills Literary Contest and Penumbra Poetry and Haiku Contest for several years as a committee of one. After working as a team of four to accomplish all the tasks Bruce has tackled single-handedly for all these years, the 2020–2021 Contest Committee members are now cognizant of the incredible amount of work he did. We are proud to honor Bruce with this dedication for his herculean task.

Thank you, Bruce. We truly appreciate you, your leadership, and your guidance.

Lyla Ellzey and Saundra Kelley, Co-Chairs
Bob Gibbs and M.R. Street, Committee Members
Seven Hills Contest Committee 2020–2021

Foreword

The Seven Hills Literary Contest and Penumbra Poetry and Haiku Contest is an annual project of the Tallahassee Writers Association. The winners of each year's contest are published in the following year's *Seven Hills Review* anthology. All entry screening, manuscript preparation, artwork, and other contributions are volunteer efforts of the Tallahassee Writers Association. The judges provide their expertise with no compensation other than a complimentary copy of the anthology. We thank the readers, judges, and all the team members profusely.

The decision of which categories to include in the contest is made each year prior to the contest opening for entries. Categories planned to be included in the 2021 Call for Entries are described at the back of this volume. For the latest information on entering and entry criteria, be sure to check for updates at **www.twaonline.org**.

This year, despite priorities lying elsewhere as we all concentrated on keeping safe and healthy, the contest received 280 entries across eight categories. The category-specific readers and judges were hard pressed to determine the winners from among the many deserving entries.

To our winning authors, CONGRATULATIONS! And to all our submitters, thank you for writing, polishing, and submitting your work. We hope you participate again next year!

A final note: If you are not already a member of Tallahassee Writers Association, please consider joining. You can check out the benefits of membership at: https://twaonline.org/.

Contents

Dedication...v

Foreword vi

The Judging Process ix

The Seven Hills Literary Competition 1

    Ten-Minute Plays...3
    1st – *COVID 29* – Tom Cavanaugh 3
    2nd – *First Folio* – Kenneth Robbins.........................16
    3rd – *Roughing It* – Judy Klass................................27

    Flash Fiction..39
    1st – *Greatest of All Time* – Richard Key 39
    2nd – *The Path Unfolding* – Lori Goshert....................41
    3rd – *Sticks and Stones* – Imago Mana 43

    Short Stories...45
    1st – *The Summer Game* – Christine Venzon 45
    2nd – *Recovery* – Yvonne Hazelton 53
    3rd – *White Swan* – Marina Brown............................59

    Adult Novel Excerpts..69
    1st – *Sisters in Exile* – Betty Cotter 69
    2nd – *Wildwind* – Lauren Strach.............................80
    3rd – *White Cloud Free* – Peter Johnson 90

    Young Adult Novel Excerpts 101
    1st – *Dark White* – Ruth Andrews...........................101
    2nd – *Coronation* – Laura Thompson 108
    3rd – *Wild and Precious Life* – Kathleen Laufenberg.......119

    Nonfiction/Creative Nonfiction 129
    1st – *Deeper than African Soil* – Faith Eidse 129
    2nd – *Blue is Truth* – Robin Storey Dunn.................140
    3rd – *A Daughter in Pieces* – Nancy Hill.................150

The Penumbra Poetry and Haiku Competition 161

   Poetry 163

   1st – *Lillian* – Sharon Yencharis 163

   2nd – *The Gardener* – Claire Scott 165

   3rd – *Shorelines* – Robert Gibbs 167

   Haiku 169

   1st – *Yesterday* – M. Shayne Bell 169

   2nd (Tie) – *Memories of elementary school* –
      Renee Szostek 170

   2nd (Tie) – *Day on the Bay* – M.R. Street 171

2020 Winning Authors 173

2020 Judges 181

2020 Reading Committee 187

2021 Competition Open Call for Submissions 189

   Seven Hills Literary Contest 189

   Penumbra Poetry and Haiku Contest 190

The Judging Process

Judging is a three-step process. First, the Contest Committee determines if entries meet the eligibility requirements. All judging is blind; we have to ensure that no preference is shown to submitters known to our readers and judges. Therefore, any entries with names attached to the primary submission were disqualified.

The second step involves a cadre of readers who sift out the top entries in each category. Our readers are all volunteers, drawn from the members of Tallahassee Writers Association and our community of readers and writers. They donated countless hours reading submissions and giving a yes, maybe, or no verdict on each submission in their category(ies).

The entries with the highest combined reader scores were sent to the finalist judges. Our 2020 judges were selected for their particular expertise, experience, and standing in their specific category. Our finalist judges used a set of criteria to score the top entries in their category. They were also given freedom to add to scores that exhibited qualities not captured in the scoring criteria.

Submissions came from near and far, with entries from 14 states and France. Haiku and Poetry again garnered the highest number of entries, with 109 and 68 entries respectively. Short Stories received 28 entries, and our newest category, Ten-Minute Plays, received 25 entries. Nonfiction/Creative Nonfiction received 15 entries, while Flash Fiction received 14 entries, and Adult Novel Excerpt received 13. Young Adult Novel Excerpt received the fewest entries with eight. We think you'll agree that the winning entries are of the highest merit.

Readers and judges, we thank you all for your professionalism and for donating your expert services to the production of this anthology. Congratulations to all our winners.

THE SEVEN HILLS
LITERARY COMPETITION

Ten-Minute Plays

Judge — Paul Donnelly
Tallahassee, Florida
"These [entries] were all engaging."

First Place
COVID 29
Tom Cavanaugh — Edison, New Jersey

TIME: 2029
PLACE: Somewhere in the U.S.A.

CAST OF CHARACTERS

JAX — Anyone Who Identifies as Female, 20s, Any Race. A strong willed, open minded, but tough woman who has never had the virus.

VROMAN — Anyone Who Identifies as male, 20s, Any Race. A shifty, opinionated, manipulative, drug dealer and raver.

Scene 1

VROMAN's bedroom.

There is a box spring and mattress on the floor at center. That is the bed. The room is messy, there are posters on the wall above the bed. JAX is asleep in the bed, her head at the foot of the bed. VROMAN is sleeping the opposite way. JAX rolls to one side and her arm dangles over the mattress and her hand hits the floor. Soon as her fingers hit the floor, JAX asks...

JAX

What time is it?

No response. JAX looks around and notices the light coming through the window.

JAX

Shit!!! Shit!!! You didn't set the alarm? OH SHIT! Why didn't the...

JAX crosses to the digital clock and looks at it.

JAX

NIGHT! PM!!! YOU SET IT FOR PM!!!!
VROMAN starts to wake up.

VROMAN

Take it easy...Calm down.

JAX

I have to go back. I have to be back. You so screwed us...

VROMAN

It's a mistake. Relax.

JAX

I have to make the noon Head Count. I have to be accountable.

VROMAN

I'll drive you to the Short Cut. You can still sneak in.

JAX is tying up her work boots.

JAX

The Scanners are awake. The Scanners are out on the street.

VROMAN

Yeah, my streets. These streets. I know they're out there on the street, but if I'm driving you, they won't stop you or pick you up if you're in a car. It's early enough. You can make it back.

JAX

I've never been out after sunrise. I don't want to get caught. I don't want to get...

VROMAN

I've gotten people back to Compound before...even in the sunlight.

JAX

Calming down

Not me. I've never been out after daybreak.

VROMAN

It's still the same world.

JAX

My world is different than your world.

VROMAN

Stop freakin...

JAX

It's the first of the month. I don't make the tally for my house, we don't get the Relief Packages.

VROMAN

If they short your package, I'll give you money.

JAX

It's not about the money.

VROMAN

Stop.

JAX

I don't make the count and they'll investigate.

VROMAN

You'll make the count.

JAX

If I don't, they'll know that I'm sneaking out.

VROMAN

I thought your people know?

JAX

Two of my friends. Two! Not my parents. Not my little sister. I have a family.

VROMAN

Think they haven't figured it out?

Silence

Relax...I've gotten other Cleans back into Compound after sun up.

JAX

Other Clean GIRLS...right? Why don't you just say it?

Silence

How many?

Silence

How many Clean Girls have you snuck back in the daytime?

Vroman smirks as he reaches for a Tee-Shirt that's on the floor.

JAX

How many more Clean girls have you gotten back in the dark? I bet it's three times as many at night than it is during the day.

VROMAN

If I tell you the number of girls, will you stop sneaking out? Will you stop coming here?

JAX

The number doesn't matter... I don't care about that. I come here for me.

VROMAN

(Grabs at her pulls her back down to the mattress)

You come here for sex....

JAX

I come here for the parties....

VROMAN

And when the night's over...you come here for the sex.

JAX pushes VROMAN away.

JAX

I come here for the p....

VROMAN

Pills?

"Pills" catches Jax off guard.

JAX

Pills are my other escape.

VROMAN

If you couldn't trip, would you still come here?

JAX

Plasmoids...have way better parties than us, Cleans.

VROMAN

That's 'cause Plasmoids know more about life and death.

JAX

That's a shitty thing to say.

VROMAN

It's the truth. We've had the Rona. We know the power of this thing.

JAX

Only power you have...is that you know...that they can't find a vaccine without you.

VROMAN

Jealous?

JAX

Maybe?

VROMAN

Why? Cleans are the protected ones.

JAX

You think that makes it easier to live?

VROMAN

You've never had it. Your family never had it. Your Compound is protected.

JAX

Protected from you...the Plasmoids...the infected.

VROMAN

Don't look at me. I didn't create the system.

JAX

We have no freedom. They keep us there saying they're keeping us safe, but...they've stripped us of our freedom...our rights...

VROMAN

All in the name of keeping you safe. Keeping Cleans safe. They don't mention us...we're expendable.

JAX

Safe isn't living. Being confined to a thirty-five-mile radius... isn't life...it's internment.

VROMAN

At least they care about you...they don't care if a Plasmoid lives or dies after they've drained all the plasma out of us! Once our bodies stop making plasma...they don't care about us. You Cleans are the chosen ones. You Cleans are the protected ones. That's why in twenty-twenty-five they started that whole Re-Settlement bullshit!

He walks away from her and looks out the window.

VROMAN

Once our plasma dries up...our blood ain't pure...and we're no good to them without it.

JAX

Does that happen?

VROMAN

They don't care if we die?

JAX

Can your body just stop making it?

VROMAN

Yeah.

JAX

Are you still making plasma?

VROMAN

Last month I was. Won't know until next month when I go back to the clinic.

JAX

What will they do?

VROMAN

No plasma?

JAX

Yeah.

VROMAN

There's rumors that they intentionally shoot the Rona back into your blood stream.

JAX

What?

VROMAN

Yeah...I've heard they purposely...get you sick again.

JAX

That could kill you.

VROMAN

Less people...less problems...

JAX

Jesus...

VROMAN

Jesus, got nothing to do with it. They are selecting who lives and dies.

JAX

They?

VROMAN

The government.

JAX

I hate them.

VROMAN

Why? They're the ones protecting you.

JAX

I'm here...doesn't that show you...I don't care about them and their shit.

VROMAN

And that's why you're here?

JAX

I told you...I'm here for me.

VROMAN

That doesn't explain why you chance getting the virus and why you chance getting caught.

JAX

I'm twenty-three years old...I want to do, what I want to do AND...I don't want them telling me what to do.

VROMAN

I'm a year older than you...and you know what I want?

JAX

No, what?

VROMAN

Stick out your arm.

JAX extends her right arm and VROMAN extends his right arm. JAX has bar code tattoo just above her wrist.

JAX

What?

VROMAN

The difference between you and me. If I had one of them, I'd be taken care of...I wouldn't have to work. They'd send me and my family The Stimulus Packages. We wouldn't need for anything. They take care of you, and me.... They leave us to fend for ourselves as they drain our blood for the plasma that may or may not create a vaccine.

JAX

You can drive to the ocean. You can live in the mountains. You can go where you want and do what you want. I live in a walled city. I have to have this...

She raises her right arm, showing the tattoo.

I have to have this scanned once a day to make sure I'm in the area I belong in. Living in the Compound isn't a privilege.

VROMAN

You're so privileged, and you don't even know it.

JAX

I didn't choose this.

VROMAN

Do you think I did?

Silence.

Why are you really here?

JAX

I told you...I'm here for...

VROMAN

"I'm here for me." You keep saying that, but...what does it really mean? Why are you really here?

JAX

I can't be late. You have to drive me back to the Short Cut, it's too late to walk it.

VROMAN takes a bottle off his dresser and tosses it to JAX. She catches the bottle and shakes it.

JAX

That's a lot of pills.

VROMAN

You're gonna need them.

JAX

This many? What are you talking about?

VROMAN

I'm not taking you back. Find your own way home.

JAX

What...why?

VROMAN

I'm sick of you privileged little Clean girls...coming under the wall...using us for what we have...getting what you need and running home to your little Clean Kingdom. All of you always crying about the freedoms you don't have when all you are is free and just don't know it.

JAX looks around, grabs an empty beer bottle and throws it at VROMAN's head.

JAX

Bastard!!!

VROMAN

Mockingly...calm, but mocking.

Tick Tock, Tick Tock, time's wasting... Tick Tock, Tick Tock... time is running out. How you gonna make it past the Scanner Patrols with that tattoo that they scan and tells them where you should be and who you are...Tick Tock, Tick Tock...and with a bottle of illegal pharmaceuticals on you...poor little Clean girl...who's gonna help you now?

JAX

Fuck you, Plasmoid!

VROMAN

Fuck you, Clean girl!

JAX

I don't need your help...I don't need anyone's help...especially, some Plasmoid Boy.

She crosses to the door and opens it.

Next time you trap a Clean in your house to mess with them...even kidnap them...the next time you're gonna pay more attention to them cause this little Clean girl definitely outsmarted you and the next one...you won't let this happen again.

VROMAN

Let what happen again?

JAX reaches into her pocket and takes out a set of car keys.

JAX

I got your car keys...Plasmoid BITCH!

JAX runs out of the room, slamming the door behind her.

VROMAN

Calm but through his teeth.

Dirty, little, Clean...

VROMAN picks up the phone and dials.

VROMAN

Hello? Yeah, I want to report my car stolen.

Blackout.

Second Place
First Folio
Kenneth Robbins — Ruston, LA

TIME: JUNE, 2016

CAST:

THE FOLIO (voice over)

A TECHNICIAN

COXMIRE, a thief

GORDY, another thief

> *At rise: a room in a library. There are shelves, books, wall hangings, tables, and a pedestal on which resides a large ancient book protected by a glass covering: this is one of the remaining original prints of Shakespeare's First Folio. It is open to* Hamlet. *The room is brightly lit. Beginning as the lights rise is the following message:*

FOLIO

William Shakespeare's First Folio is on loan from the Folger Shakespearean Library, Washington, DC, for the month of June to commemorate the 400th year since the author's death. The public is invited to view the text during —

(blip)

William Shakespeare's First Folio is on loan from the Folger Shakespearean Library, Washington, DC, for the month of June to commemorate the 400th year since the author's death. The public is invited to view the text during —

(blip)

William Shakespeare's First Folio is on loan from the Folger Shakespearean Library, Washington, DC, for the month of June to commemorate the 400th year since the author's death. The public is invited to view the text during –

There is a strange electronic sound and the message stops. A TECHNICIAN rises from behind the FOLIO's podium and speaks into a walkie-talkie.

TECHNICIAN

Yo, boss?

(there is static)

Can't fix it tonight. Gonna take some rewiring, maybe even shutting the whole thing down for a day or two. There's a glitch and I can't fix it tonight. We're closed for the evening anyway. So I shut it down.

(more static)

No, I can't. Just one of those things. You know how things like this work. If it's gonna break, it's gonna break. I'll fix it tomorrow, boss, no problem. Tomorrow. 10-4. Over and out.

(replaces her walkie-talkie and speaks to the Folio)

Stupid, sonofabitching fancy thingamagig. One big headache, that's what you are. Jesus.

She leaves, stopping at the entry to turn out all the lights. Total darkness. A faint light rises from the Folio, the only light in the room.

FOLIO

To be...or not to be...that is the....

The door opens and light from outside the room floods in. The Folio light fades out as two shadowy figures enter. Both are dressed in

17

black. They close the door, gently, quietly. Darkness. The only light comes from their hand-held flashlights.

COXMIRE

Shhhhhhh....

GORDY

Shhhhh yaself. I ain't said nothing.

A beam from a flashlight stops on the Folio's podium.

COXMIRE

There it is.

GORDY

That's it?

COXMIRE

That's it.

GORDY

Don't look like much to me.

COXMIRE

That book's worth a million dollars.

GORDY

No book's worth a million dollars.

COXMIRE

Well, this one is.

GORDY

How come?

COXMIRE

It's Shakespeare, stupid.

GORDY

I know what it is. You don't have to call me stupid.

COXMIRE

Wow. Can't believe I'm actually looking at it.

(leaning over it, sniffing)

Smelling it.

GORDY

It's under glass, ya dolt. You can't smell squat when it's under glass.

COXMIRE

Wish I could touch it.

GORDY

Well, you'll have to touch it if we go through with your plan.

COXMIRE

Not yet. Give it time.

GORDY

It ain't gonna bite you.

COXMIRE

It's smaller than I thought.

GORDY

Looks big enough to me. Bet it weights ten pounds.

COXMIRE

Eighteen. That's what the website says.

GORDY

Fat bugger. Let's bag it and get out of here.

COXMIRE

Some things shouldn't be rushed.

GORDY

And this is one of them?

COXMIRE

It's the mother of them all.

(as Gordy reaches toward the book)

Don't touch it. It may be wired.

He investigates the podium as Gordy shines his flashlight on the other books in the room.

GORDY

How come these books ain't under glass?

COXMIRE

They ain't Shakespeare.

GORDY

I read some of a Shakespeare play back in junior high. This horny teenager falls in love with a chick then kills another guy and gets exiled or something. Everybody dies in the end. Bummer.

COXMIRE

You never learned to read.

GORDY

Well, the teacher told us all about it. It was in poetry. Hate damn poetry.

COXMIRE

Okay, looks like it's wired to some sort of alarm system. But somebody turned it off.

GORDY

How you know it's turned off?

COXMIRE

There's a warning light, see? Here? And it ain't on. The system's been turned off. You got your screw driver?

GORDY

Here.

COXMIRE

Hold my light for me.

He unscrews the protective covering and lifts it to the floor.

GORDY

How do you know you're not setting off an alarm somewhere else in the building?

COXMIRE

I don't.

GORDY

How do you know the cops ain't busting in here in a minute now?

COXMIRE

I don't.

GORDY

We should get our asses out of here, Cox. We must be stupid, stealing a million dollar book. Jeez, smells like mold.

COXMIRE

It's been locked under glass for almost four hundred years. Smell that. It's breathing.

GORDY

Can we get out of here now?

COXMIRE

(entranced by the book)

When I was in 10th grade, we read *Macbeth*. Awesome story. Witches, murders, a blood bath. Anyway, my teacher, Ms. Shehane, was full of Shakespeare stuff. Strange, weird stuff.

GORDY

Like what?

COXMIRE

Well, for one, actors never say the name of Macbeth in a theater. You do? Somebody's gonna get his head chopped off before dawn. Maybe your own. That sort of thing.

GORDY

Stupid. You don't believe that kind of superstition stuff, do you?

COXMIRE

Don't know. I ain't an actor. But if I was, I might.

(reaches to touch the book but pulls back)

Ms. Shehane, she also told us that where Shakespeare is buried, somewhere in Scotland, that nobody's robbed his tomb.

GORDY

Why not?

COXMIRE

There's a curse on his remains. Anybody who disturbs his bones or something like that, well, they're gonna die some horrible death.

GORDY

This damn teacher of yours really got your goat, ain't she.

COXMIRE

I dropped out of school after reading Macbeth. Just about did me in.

(reaches to touch the book again but again withdraws)

GORDY

You scared of it or something?

COXMIRE

There was something else Ms. Shehane told us. Something really scary.

GORDY

Okay, you got me going. What was it?

COXMIRE

She said: anybody who touches an original copy of the First Folio will be transformed.

GORDY

(wait for it)

How?

COXMIRE

Made instantly into the smartest person on the planet.

GORDY

Jesus. Can't stand smart people. Nerds, every one of them.

COXMIRE

Yeah. Hate smart people. But that was what she told us. Touch it and be transformed.

GORDY

Well, that's just plain stupid.

COXMIRE

You got that right, Gordy baby.

He touches the FOLIO. Its light, faint, begins to glow.

FOLIO

To be....

COXMIRE immediately moves away. He has dropped his flashlight. GORDY turns his beam onto COXMIRE's face, revealing a sudden transformation.

COXMIRE

Did you hear?

GORDY

I didn't hear nothing.

COXMIRE

I am afrighted but I know not why.

GORDY

For Christ's sake, let's take this thing and get the hell out of here.

COXMIRE

I have had a rare vision.

GORDY

Yeah, right. It ain't gonna work on me, fella, you know that?

COXMIRE

I have had a dream, past the wit of man to say what dream it was. Man is but an ass if he go about to expound this dream.

GORDY

What the hell are you talking about?

COXMIRE

The eye of man hath not heard, the ear of man hath not seen,
man's hand is not able to taste, his tongue to conceive, nor his
heart to report what my dream was.

GORDY

This ain't funny, Coxmire.

COXMIRE

If we shadows have offended,
Think but this, and all is mended,
That you have but slumbered here
While these visions did appear.

GORDY

Enough with the Visions! Let's take this thing and scat!

He touches the FOLIO. Again, the FOLIO's light fades up.

FOLIO

Or not to be....

*GORDY steps away, dropping his flashlight which COXMIRE
fetches for him.*

COXMIRE

Give me your hands if we be friends—

GORDY

Why have you suffered me to be imprisoned,
Kept in a dark house
And made the most notorious geck and gull
That e'er invention played on?

COXMIRE

I know not why.

GORDY

Nor do I. Now is the winter of our discontent. From hence we must flee. Anon, anon, I prithee, anon.

He exits running.

COXMIRE

No more words! Away! Go, away!

He exits. Total darkness. The FOLIO's light rises.

FOLIO

To die, to sleep, perchance to dream...

The door opens and the TECHNICIAN returns, her pistol drawn. She turns on the overhead light and, seeing that the room is empty, speaks over her walkie-talkie.

TECHNICIAN

Yes, sir? False alarm. Nobody here. Yeah, you can turn off the alarm now. Yes, sir, got it taken care of. 10-4. Over and out.

She is leaving when she notices that the protective cover has been removed from the pedestal. She scratches her head, then lifts the cover to return it to its place. But as she does so, the light from the FOLIO returns.

FOLIO

...Perchance to dream. Ay, there's the rub...

The TECHNICIAN touches the book and immediately withdraws, a look of awe coming over her face. She staggers toward the entry and stands with her hand on the light switch.

TECHNICIAN

Tomorrow, and tomorrow, and tomorrow... Creepy.

She turns off the light and shuts the door.

Blackout.

Third Place
Roughing It
Judy Klass — Nashville, Tennessee

SETTING:

A yard so big it is almost a field.

CAST

MICHELLE, in her 40s or 50s

DAVE, in his 40s or 50s

INGRID, 18

KAYLA, a younger teen

Lights up on an outdoor scene: the family is in the area of their sleeping bags in a yard so big, it's almost a field.

MICHELLE is handing her husband and daughters trail mix. She and DAVE seem happy and excited in a way that is almost forced. INGRID may be helping them along with that. KAYLA is not into it.

MICHELLE

Here's a little trail mix. Gorp, we used to call it at camp.

INGRID

Thanks, Mom. It's good.

MICHELLE

It's just so nice of Alan and his family to do this for us.

(To DAVE)

How long have you known him again?

DAVE

Oh, Alan and I go way back.

MICHELLE

Kindergarten?

DAVE

Well. Not quite. Third grade, I guess. We were in the Boy Scouts together. Cub Scouts and Boy Scouts.

MICHELLE

Really?

DAVE

Sure. And that's where we both learned about the fun of camping out.

KAYLA

Yeah? So, how come him and his family aren't out here?

DAVE

He's keeping his eye on what we're doing. He says it's exciting, and they might try it also, next spring.

KAYLA

Are they keeping an eye on us from their window up there?

MICHELLE

Kayla, don't be nasty—it's really nice for the Dunnings to let us use their backyard.

DAVE

You can see they've got the shades down, Kayla. So, no, they're not watching us that way. I just meant—Alan wants me to check in with him and report on the experiment. Tell them how it's going.

INGRID

It's a big yard. It's like a field, out here in the country. I mean, you can almost forget that the house is back there.

DAVE

That's the spirit. And with the trees, and all this space...we don't have to worry about nosy neighbors. We've got our own little wonderland out here.

KAYLA

But you're paying them. Right? It's not like they said: come, camp out in our big backyard! For free! Bring your sleeping bags! Use the bathroom in the pool house!

DAVE

We're paying 'em $200 a month, yes.

KAYLA

Why? Why do this at all?

DAVE

It's an experiment. We're trying something out.

KAYLA

But if we don't like it tonight, can we go do something normal?

INGRID

Kayla, come on, we're here now, let's give it a chance.

KAYLA

Ingrid, I cannot believe you. I can't believe you want to be part of this insanity.

INGRID

Whatever. Mom and Dad are into trying this. I figure I'll keep an open mind. Were you in the Girl Scouts, Mom?

MICHELLE

No, scouting was more your father's thing. Did you go on overnight trips a lot, Dave?

DAVE

Sure. Sometimes we were in tents. And sometimes we were sleeping under the stars, like we'll be doing tonight.

MICHELLE

Did you tell each other ghost stories?

DAVE

Oh, there's always one guy who's got the flashlight glowing in the dark, trying to scare everyone with stories.

MICHELLE

Did you earn merit badges?

DAVE

I got one or two.

INGRID

Can you, like, tie different kinds of knots?

DAVE

I used to be able to, yeah. A slip knot. A sheepshank. I tell you, I'm no Eagle Scout. But I learned some good life lessons from scouting. I got some practical skills. And you learn about roughing it. You end up a little less soft. You learn a little more of what it takes to survive.

KAYLA

Okay, Dad, but...we're not finding our way home from a forest by following the tree bark, or moss, or whatever. I mean—we're camping out in somebody's big backyard. It's—it's weird.

DAVE

Can you smell the grass, Kayla, and the earth? Can you hear—

KAYLA

And suddenly, we're just going to "live" here? I mean, it's—bizarre. How does this teach us life lessons?

MICHELLE

It's family time. We used to go on camping trips when Ingrid was little.

INGRID

I remember, Mom.

MICHELLE

And we haven't done it in a while. But I think it'll bring us together. Talking to each other. Experiencing nature a little, without all of us off in different rooms, watching TV or playing with our phones. I think we'll end up closer as a family.

KAYLA

Fine. So, why don't we go to a hotel, and keep the TV and our phones switched off? And have deep discussions?

INGRID

Kayla, don't be a jerk. We're here now, so let's try this.

MICHELLE

Think of it as summer vacation, baby.

KAYLA

I'm *on* summer vacation. Even if I have to find a McJob.

MICHELLE

Then, think of it as a family trip.

KAYLA

To the Dunnings' backyard?

MICHELLE

Think of it as an adventure.

DAVE

Think of it as an adventure in outdoor barbecue! You kids have never had my flame-broiled burgers, I guess.

INGRID

No, I have. I remember, Dad.

DAVE

Well, Alan's got a pretty amazing grill over there. I'm gonna start calling it my fire pit. And once I get the hang of it, you're both gonna be thinking of your old man as a premium chef. Of course, this first time using it is gonna be the challenge...

MICHELLE

Would you like me to help you with it, Dave? I'd like to learn my way around it also.

DAVE

Okay, great. You girls hungry?

INGRID

Getting there, Dad.

DAVE

Great. Michelle, let's go take a look.

MICHELLE

You got the matches?

DAVE

They're already over there…

(MICHELLE and DAVE exit in the direction of a barbecue grill in the other part of the yard. KAYLA, annoyed, turns on her older sister.)

KAYLA

Ingrid, what is your problem?

INGRID

What do you mean?

KAYLA

Why are you acting like this is okay? Like this is normal?

INGRID

I think we should both act like this is okay. I think we should try to make Mom and Dad feel good about it.

KAYLA

When they're losing their minds?

INGRID

They're scared. They're doing the best they can.

KAYLA

I don't care. I want to go home. I wish we hadn't left. I wish they worked something out with the landlord. I'd like to go to sleep in my room.

INGRID

It's not our house anymore. It's a lucky break that Dad's friend is letting us store so much of our stuff in containers in the pool house.

KAYLA

But why move out before we had a new place to go? Why were Mom and Dad not even *looking* for a house?

INGRID

Kayla, don't you get it? Come on. Do you really not understand what's going on?

KAYLA

What are you...

INGRID

We didn't "move out," okay? We were basically thrown out. If we'd stayed another day, the men might have shown up to throw our stuff onto the street. They probably came today and changed the locks.

KAYLA

Seriously?

INGRID

It's not ours anymore, so forget it. Did you seriously not get the memo? Are you not registering—

KAYLA

Mom and Dad didn't say—

INGRID

Mom and Dad don't want us to know that they can't pay the rent? All right? They had money in the bank, and then Mom had that operation last year, and the savings were wiped out. And then—ever since the company laid Dad off, both of them have been freaking out. And Mom's salary is not enough. And Dad hasn't been able to find something.

KAYLA

Okay, but this is insane. Sleeping in these people's backyards, like we're hippies or something? Nobody does this.

INGRID

Well, it was either this or a homeless shelter.

KAYLA

Homeless shelter.

INGRID

Yeah, Kayla, we're homeless. Deal with it. But Mom and Dad don't want us to know that we're homeless. They don't want that stigma. That might traumatize us. So, they're acting all hearty and happy, and they've made up this wonderful family adventure story.

KAYLA

Seriously?

INGRID

Yeah. I've been eavesdropping on some pretty intense conversations. They tried to see if we could move in with Aunt Amy, but she and Mom kind of hate each other. They've been looking into different things, and this is what they came up with. They're terrified, and they don't know what to do...

KAYLA

We're homeless people?

INGRID

More or less. So, when they talk about roughing it, and survival skills... It's kind of true. Even if we're sleeping in somebody's big old backyard. We maybe have to get tough, and help them, and not let them know we know. I wasn't going to tell you, but you're being a pain and a brat, and you keep whining—

KAYLA

I didn't know!

INGRID

I think maybe you chose not to know. You thought they just randomly went with sleeping in someone's yard instead of a hotel?

KAYLA

I want to go home.

INGRID

I think we need to grow up, fast. And be strong for them, and act happy. And get summer jobs, if possible, or at least babysit, and meanwhile, they're saving money, and Dad's taking the bus and Lyft rides to job interviews—he might find something. He's giving this place as his address. You should do the same. And maybe we can rent a new house or apartment, or we wind up in a double-wide, but until then—

KAYLA

What if it rains?

INGRID

They bought that tent. It's supposed to be waterproof.

KAYLA

What if it's not? What if it gets really cold?

INGRID

Then—maybe we crowd into the pool house. Or the Dunnings' basement. And we find a way to get through this.

KAYLA

Ingrid, you have seriously...you have seriously turned my world upside down.

INGRID

Don't let them know you know.

(MICHELLE and DAVE return.)

DAVE

Okay, people! We've got the grill fired up. And the question is: what do you want on your burgers?

INGRID

What are the options?

DAVE

American cheese! Lettuce! Tomatoes! Salt! Pepper! Sesame bun!

KAYLA

That sounds good, Dad.

INGRID

Definitely.

DAVE

How well cooked do you like your burger?

KAYLA

Medium.

INGRID

I like mine well done.

DAVE

We aim to please!

MICHELLE

And then, after dinner, we can roast marshmallows over the grill—I really think that will work. When I was a kid at camp, I loved marshmallow roasts. If it works, we can try making smores...

KAYLA

That sounds great!

MICHELLE

It seems like you're feeling a little better about this, Kayla.

DAVE

Yeah, really, kiddo. I'm glad to see that.

INGRID

Well, like you said, you used to take me camping. So, I gave her a pep talk about it.

KAYLA

She did, and I'm into it now. I'm psyched. Let's have a family adventure!

Lights Down

Flash Fiction

Judge — Anna Yeatts
Pinehurst, North Carolina
"My congratulations to all the winners (and participants)!... It's always an honor to read for [the Seven Hills Contest]."

First Place
Greatest of All Time
Richard Key — Dothan, Alabama

Harold was a recluse, but he did not want that to define him. He would rather be defined by his contributions to society. Nevertheless, the "Nobody's Home" sign on the door was what most people equated with the man.

Yard work was a perennial problem for Harold since it either required dealing with someone who could do the work, or actually going outside and doing it himself. But this conundrum was solved when Harold went on e-Bay and bought a goat for forty-nine dollars. Unfortunately, the shipping was $386, about what a Honda would cost, even though he would never have spent that much on a mower, even if it came with GPS, Bluetooth, and awesome cup-holders.

He named the goat Matilda, hoping it was a she-goat and not a billy goat. He never bothered to look. Matilda did not share Harold's love of the indoors, preferring to roam the exterior of the house ingesting whatever she (or he) felt like.

And the yard never looked nicer, or at least, the grass never looked shorter, like the shorn heads of young men who shave their scalps to obscure the reality of hair loss.

So Harold was able to remain a recluse. He had a post office box he only visited once a week, after dark on Sunday evening. That way he could come home and sort his mail while sitting in his easy chair watching reruns of *The Big Valley* on MeTV. He had a thing for Barbara Stanwyck's character, Victoria Barkley, a strong handsome woman, but despised the placid and taciturn Heath.

Matilda was not a free-range goat. She had to be tied up to a tree or a post at various spots around the yard to allow a uniform appearance to the vegetation. This goat relocation Harold performed early in the morning before the neighbors went outside to look for their newspaper or walk their insistent little house dogs. The neighbors began to refer to Harold's house as "the goat house," and the little dogs spent excessive energy barking their disapproval at the funny-looking cat.

Harold had recently had a reversal of fortune despite his personality quirks. Long ago he was instrumental in crafting messages for the outside of unsolicited mail, like URGENT! Open Immediately! Check Enclosed! But after the technology revolution, his services were less in demand. After a few lean years, though, he made the transition, and was now able to make a living bothering people on-line, flooding their in-boxes with quick cures for everything from psoriasis to ringing in the ears and quick fixes for vision defects. Soon he was authoring eye-catching headlines such as Four Poisons You Eat Every Day and Seven Foods You Should Never Feed Your Children. Harold was a quick study and was on his way to spam superstardom.

But one very dark morning, Harold tripped over Matilda's tether and got a subdural hematoma. Then Matilda ate Harold's pants.

Second Place
The Path Unfolding
Lori Goshert — Tallahassee, Florida

A shrill whistle quickens your steps as you make your way through the crush of bodies, the scent of someone's woody aftershave mingling with the smell of fresh bread from the bakery.

You heft your bags up the train's narrow steps and find a dusty cabin—your refuge for the nine-hour journey. You left the wreckage of your previous life and fled to the Balkans. A war-torn region for your war-torn self.

As the train pulls out of the city, you mull over the previous day. You savored your new-found independence, exploring Zagreb with its cathedral and mosque, its monuments and parks with peeling sycamores, and returned to the snug, music-themed hotel. You had a good cry on the quilted bed and a refreshing night's sleep. The clouds began to roll away, revealing a sliver of light by which you got a faint glimpse of a future, a fresh path of your own choosing. The past was becoming blurred at the edges, like something you had read in a book.

It is unseasonably warm. Even the weather is cheering you onward. Yesterday, you walked among the people as if you belonged. You flowed through the crowd as they stared straight ahead, clutching their phones and groceries. You hope you will be accepted in your temporary home. Is your memory still young enough to retain a new language?

The view snaps you out of your reverie. Your breath catches as the soft hills loom into view, and now you are in the valley. A filmy mist rings the green hills, pierced with still-bare trees.

Below them, farmland spreads in rectangles—tan, dark brown, yellow-green, and emerald. Smoke billows from the chimneys of red and white brick farmhouses with dark shingles. You wonder who lives in them and what their lives are like— whether they are happy in this countryside, surrounded by so much beauty but having to do back-breaking work from sunup to sunset. You wonder whether you could be happy with such a life, and you are honest enough to say "no."

The river appears on your left, shimmering and winding in the late afternoon sun like a serpent. You check the map—it is the Sava. The hills undulate against a slate-blue sky as the train speeds past. Your breathing has become more regular and your anxiety has fallen away. You press your palm to the cool glass, longing to use all your senses to absorb this unfamiliar landscape.

You continue to stare out the window, straining to see long after the sun has sunk below the horizon. Finally, you settle back into your seat and close your eyes. In the darkness, you see the universe and time stretched out before you, deep red and boundless. They tried to suffocate you but didn't know you carried your liberation inside. You choose your path forward and open your eyes. The train thunders along the tracks, carrying you into the future.

Third Place
Sticks and Stones
Imago Mana — Pahoa, Hawaii

As the cold steel doors to the coal bin were heaved open, we watched in awe. Most of us gathered around the twice a week ritual like morbid curiosity seekers surrounding a satanic ritual simultaneously frightened and fascinated. The familiar sound of the coal-laden dump truck rumbling closer was an invitation for me to edge my way through the other children up to the front of the crowd.

To us, this was not about heating. Our young minds conjured up images of untold evils taking place in the bowels of our apartment building, led by the coal men. Blackened with coal dust, they scurried about the underground corridors filling us with unfounded fear whenever they approached. As I neared the front row of the mob, my nose caught the faint but familiar odor of the black dust mingling with their sweat. I stopped. I was close enough to reach out and graze the shovel in one of the coal men's hands. I took comfort in the fact that although small, the little boy I stood behind was a barrier between myself and the soot-covered workers as they unhooked the chains and raised the truck bed.

We covered our ears during the thunderous roar of the rusty truck bestowing its gift of gleaming, ebony rocks. Within seconds the gaping mouth of the coal bin had swallowed every last morsel. The doors were sealed. The empty truck seemed to heave a sigh of relief as it left. While the other children raced back to their interrupted play, I ran to reclaim my throne atop the coal bin doors. Where I had ruled my kingdom before the invasion of the coal men.

Suddenly, I was overtaken by a boy intent upon overthrowing my reign.

Beaten to the throne, I indignantly demanded, "Get up, I was here first!"

"You move your feet, you lose your seat," he teased.

"Shut up!" I interrupted.

"Make me!" he dared.

"I don't make trash. I burn it." I retorted.

"No wonder you're so black!" he yelled. "At least the coal men can wash off the black."

"I'm not black!" I gasped, insulted by being compared to the much-maligned coal men.

"You're colored." He challenged, holding his pale white hand up to mine in contrast. With those words, his coup was complete as I ran crying home to Mama.

It was ironic that my first conscious encounter with prejudice happened in the midst of my own unconscious bias, arising out of my fear and ignorance of the coal men.

Wrapped up in the rude awakening that I was different from so many of the children in our military complex were lessons about the pain of bigotry, the acceptance of myself and others, regardless of our differences and the futility of the childhood adage Mama recited while she wiped my tears. "Sticks and stones may break my bones..." You know the rest.

Short Stories

Judge — Sheree Reneé Thomas
Memphis, Tennessee
"I enjoyed these stories…and I am wishing all these writers continued success."

First Place
The Summer Game
Christine Venzon — Peoria, Illinois

In the kitchen I'm canning peaches, pushed to the limit by the two industrious fruit trees in our backyard. But the real drama—the summer game, they call it—is unfolding in the living room.

It's St. Louis Cardinals at Los Angeles Dodgers. The Dodgers lead it 3-1 in the second inning. A.J. Rivera pitches for the Cardinals.

Joe Buck does the play-by-play: "Rivera gets it over the corner of the plate to even the count at a ball and a strike."

Tim McCarver analyzes: "That slider is the one pitch Rivera has thrown with success in these last few starts."

I do meta-analysis: Success, Tim? The kid has given up nine runs in seven innings in these last few starts. His team is down three to one, he has a man on third, facing a guy who's hitting .286 with men in scoring position, and it's only the second inning. Yep, that slider has made some difference. And anyway, you probably jinxed it.

The at-bat goes on. Ball. Strike. Pop foul. Joe Buck informs me that catcher Yadier Molina asks for time out. Catcher and pitcher talk strategy on the mound.

I add my own counsel: Stay focused, kid. One more out gets you out of this jam and makes one 12-year-old boy and his mom in Springfield, Illinois very happy — at least for another half-inning.

Molina's pep talk does as much good as mine. A ball and a foul tip later, Buck shouts: "Rivera uncorks a wild pitch! Molina chases it down. Greene is coming home from third! Rivera covers the plate... Safe! It's four-one Dodgers."

See — I told you. Thanks a lot, Tim.

"Now Josh Hancock is throwing in the Cardinal bullpen. It looks like that's all for Rivera."

McCarver commiserates: "Strategically, no manager wants to go to his bullpen this early. It's a tough call to make emotionally too, pulling a young pitcher who needs to rebuild confidence. It's frustrating all around, and no one is more bewildered than Rivera—"

Tim is silenced in mid-punditry. Chuck Taylor All-Stars thump across the carpet. Sean pauses long enough to throw me a glance. His dark features are clouded, like Molly our spaniel when the man from Terminix disappears into the basement to check for termites. "I'm going for a ride."

Someone is more bewildered than Rivera, Tim.

"Wear your helmet. And be careful," I warn to a slamming screen door. Frustration makes a lousy GPS.

I was afraid of this. I'd been afraid since last May, when A.J. Rivera came up from the minors, a 22-year-old pitching phenom from Triple A Memphis. Like our backyard peach trees, he promised a sweet season for Cards fans. Wicked hanging curveball. Baffling sidearm slider. He had the team on top of the standings going into the All-Star break. He pitched in the game, of course, two innings of one-hit ball.

For Sean, it was pure hero worship. Posters on his bedroom walls, Rivera's official Major League Baseball jersey on his back. The boy who struggled to solve for x in seventh-grade algebra now calculated statistics like adjusted pitching runs (innings pitched divided by nine, multiplied by the difference between league earned run average and player's earned run average). And Rivera seemed worthy of adulation, a kid with an ego and work ethic grounded in reality. Also a terrific smile. I had hoped that by the time he proved merely mortal, Sean would have a bit of seasoning himself.

Instead they were both far too green. And I was nowhere near ready.

Ten minutes later the crunch of gravel signals his return. "Feeling better?" I ask.

But stress management is a concept lost on a 12-year-old boy, like perspective and perseverance and every other grown-up "coping skill" his dad and I have urged on him during A.J. Rivera's horrific freefall. A blur of white T-shirt flies past. The kitchen door slams; the bathroom door replies. My mother's ears detect the faucet blasting—What? Do we own stock in the water company?—then the telltale creak of the medicine cabinet door.

"You all right in there?"

Silence. Then, "Yeah."

"Good. 'Cause I need your help here."

"Just a minute."

Just a minute passes, then several more. The mound of peeled peaches grows. I leave the blanching water and Fruit

Fresh and rap on the door. "Can I come in?"

I ease the door open. Sean daubs at the red, grated skin on his elbow with a cotton wad, scowling at the pain, at being caught. The sink is lined with Bactine, Neosporin, gauze pads, tape and scissors, the surgical kit he has seen me assemble since he learned to walk, it seems.

I snip a few lengths of tape and hang them from the medicine cabinet. "That's a hard spot to bandage. Leave it a little loose, it stays on better."

Sean smears a gauze square with Neosporin and slaps it on the raw spot. Not snubbing me, exactly. Just getting on with the job, man-like.

"Come out to the kitchen when you're done."

I'm reaching for the oven mitts when the bathroom door clicks. Sean addresses the bowl of peaches. "What do you want me to do?"

I try to ignore the tufts of gauze sticking out beneath a railroad track of tape on the elbow. "Take the jars out of the dishwasher and set them on the towel on the counter. Use the tongs. They're still hot."

One by one he removes the Mason jars. I pack them with peach chunks and ladle hot syrup over. Sean bends his good elbow on the counter and rests his chin in his palm.

"What's that for?"

"It keeps the peaches from getting mushy. Can you wet a paper towel and wipe the mouth of the jars? Make sure there's no syrup on them."

He cleanses the rims, then resumes his vigil as I screw on Kerr lids and rings. "Why are they in two parts?"

I explain the rationale for two-piece lids, and then for pressure-cooker processing. His interest is unusual. Sean has a boy's fascination for cooking—for mashing potatoes, pounding steak, pulverizing anything in the food processor. The whys are irrelevant.

I turn on the burner under the pressure cooker and start soaping measuring cups and mixing bowls. Sean asks: "What else can I do?"

I remember how, when he was five, he pestered his dad and me to let him help—put away groceries, mow the lawn, retile the bathroom. But now he's twelve, it's a summer Saturday afternoon, and his hero is pitching on TV. I should be pestering *him*.

I wring out a kitchen rag with instructions to find the sticky spots. He sets upon counters and tabletop, rubbing them to a state of sanitation. I give in to the motherly urge to peek beneath the bandage, check on the sore. But quickly, the way I peck his cheek before dropping him off at school: "Bummer about Rivera."

Sean scrubs the corner cabinets. "Who cares about Rivera."

I let it go, busying myself with drying dishes while Sean polishes the metal handles on the cabinets. Finally the counterweight on the pressure cooker starts to jiggle. I turn down the heat and set the timer for 25 minutes. I'm inking a roll of labels with "Peaches Aug. 4" when a hoarse, choked plea escapes behind me:

"He was going so good. What happened to him?"

I turn. Sean seems engrossed by the spice rack. He isn't asking for a cause, for a treatise on the mechanics of throwing a breaking ball. Yet he wants a reason, a reassurance to hold the universe intact, like the unbroken seam that joins the pieces of cowhide on a baseball and keeps the yarns inside from raveling —or worse yet, the core from exploding on impact.

Given that choice, I'd rather try to explain the physics of pitching. "He's probably wondering the same thing."

An honest reply, and Sean rewards me by not stomping off. Instead, groping, he relives the fateful day, the exact moment the symptoms of the dread disease appeared: "It was that first start after the All-Star game, against the Reds. The fourth inning. He walked the bases full and gave up that triple to Griffey."

I recall that shellacking. Rivera attributed it to deviating from his traditional pre-game meal: fried chicken and waffles with syrup, which he'd eaten before every start going back to his stint in Memphis. ("Even in Colorado Springs. At the IHOP.") The explanation had reassured Sean. If only it had worked.

"Maybe he's trying too hard," I suggest. "He's trying to control too much."

The idea meets with raised brows. Pitching is all about control. Lack of control—that's Rivera's problem. That's what will earn him the unspeakable humiliation of getting sent back down to the minors. Sean counters: "Maybe he's tired. He was going into the sixth inning almost every start."

"Could be. Maybe his body is trying to tell him he needs a break. All his life, it's been nothing but baseball. Morning, noon, and night. Breakfast, lunch, and dinner. Baseball, baseball, baseball."

I try to imagine what that must feel like. Since the kid was Sean's age, throwing a baseball has been more than a ticket to fame, to cheers and envy and the cover of *ESPN The Magazine*. It has defined him, has been the purpose and essence of life. Now, to feel it slipping away, while coaches and trainers and psychologists and maybe even astrologers, all probe and pry and offer their best advice...and still it keeps slipping away.

I go on: "One morning he gets up, and he's got it all working. He's on top of the world. Then suddenly, it's gone. He doesn't know why, or how, it's just gone. And he doesn't know if he'll ever get it back. What's he going to do if he doesn't?"

What the hell is he going to do?

"He must be scared out of his mind. I know I'd be."

Sean's eyes widen, just barely, as if hit by a pitch but refusing to show the sting. "Yeah."

We've roused a monster, shrewder and more frightening than anything that ever hid in Sean the six-year-old's closet. A hint, a growing unease: If the arm can fail, the physical skills perfected can up and abandon, your own body betray you, snatching away the thing you've wanted and worked for all your life, the force that held you in orbit...

What in the universe can be counted on?

And this monster never leaves. If anything, it reproduces. Like mold, bacteria. Toxins lying dormant, hidden under the lid of innocent-looking canned peaches. The terrifying realization that life is an unsecured note. What you had may be taken away. Things you believe in might not be true. People you believe in might not deserve your trust, might even abuse it.

Yet, still we can peaches.

I offer a daring suggestion. "It may not be a bad thing. If he finds out what's wrong, he could pitch even better than before. And if he doesn't, he might find something he likes to do more."

It falls as weak comic relief. Sean smirks. "Like what?"

Like falling in love and raising a child, I want to say.

"You'd be surprised."

The timer shrieks its tinny alarm. I turn off the flame and slide the pressure cooker off the burner. "There. Now we'll have summer peaches year 'round."

Sean stares at the canner. "They're not as good, though," he says, softly. "They're not, like, *real* summer peaches."

It's the lament of an August afternoon. Canning peaches is intellectually rewarding. You feel wise and capable for having saved what otherwise would have gone to waste. Eating canned peaches in January, you congratulate yourself for appreciating that they are perfectly adequate, certainly superior to anything on the supermarket shelves.

But deep down you long for the velvety skin, ruby and burgundy and gold; the flesh *al dente,* yielding yet firm enough to be savored slowly; the juice like nectar, still warm from the sun, trickling down your chin because you couldn't wait for a knife to slice it.

Summer peaches are summer itself.

"No," I admit, sighing. "Once summer peaches are gone, they're gone."

The summer game, they call it. It unfolds inning by inning, pitch by pitch.

Second Place
Recovery
Yvonne Hazelton — Paris, France

Carol shifted the vase of flowers to her other arm and pushed open the door.

Willa's IV hung from its pole at the head of the bed, her heart monitor pulsing as she slept. Her chest was uneven under her blue hospital gown, her remaining breast soft and drooping to the side, the padded wound bulky on the other. A catheter bag hung at the foot of the bed, just visible beneath the blanket.

Carol put the flowers on top of the TV where Willa would see them when she woke up. She arranged the blanket to hide the catheter bag, knowing Willa would be mortified if any visitors saw it. She was glad she'd brought Willa some new lavender-flowered pajamas. She'd help her put them on as soon as they removed the catheter. Carol had tried them on herself in Boaz's department store, and she knew they would fit since Carol and Willa were both perfect size twelves, except that Willa was one inch taller.

The door opened and the nurse came in. "Hi, Frances."

"Hi, Carol. You staying the night?" She checked the IV and the catheter bag.

"Yes. How is she?"

"Oh, she's a trooper. She's caught up on her pain meds, but you let the nurses' station know if she wakes up and needs some more."

"I will. Thank you."

Frances left, and Carol was alone with her friend.

Deciding to go ahead and settle in for the night, she washed her face in the bathroom sink and rubbed in moisturizer, brushed her teeth. It was dark outside. She dragged the armchair, as quietly as she could, from the window to the bedside, got her library book and small flashlight out of her overnight bag, and began to read. Soon, however, she realized that reading *Sophie's Choice* at the bedside of your best friend who's just had cancer surgery was too much. She put it aside. She couldn't sleep sitting up, so she lowered the bar on the near side of the bed and put her head on her arms near Willa's feet.

In the night, Carol heard a groan and felt the blanket tugging under her head. She sat up. "Willa? Are you okay? Do you need anything?"

"Need you to get off my blanket." Willa's voice was hoarse.

"Oh, I'm sorry! Here, let's get you comfortable." Carol adjusted the sheets and blankets, straightened the pillow as best she could without having Willa lift her head. "Are you thirsty? I can go get you some ice chips."

"Okay. Thanks."

Carol started for the door.

"Maybe time for some more morphine." She could hear the tightness in Willa's voice.

"Sure." Carol went to the nurses' station and told them Willa needed morphine, then went to the ice machine. She knew where it was. She had sat up nights in this hospital with her father after his heart attack, with her mother after she fell and broke her hip. She knew the routine. She knew to get only half a bucket of ice, because no one could eat a full bucket of ice before it melted. Willa probably wouldn't need even half a bucket.

When Carol got back to the room, the nurse was giving Willa a shot of morphine in the IV drip. She straightened her pillow more vigorously than Carol had dared, wrote on Willa's chart, and left the room.

"I got you some ice chips. Can I raise the bed a little?"

Willa nodded, her hair flattened at the back, a salt and pepper halo around her face. Carol cranked the head of the bed up and sat on the edge, careful not to disturb the blankets. She spooned a small ice chip into Willa's mouth, waited until Willa nodded, spooned another. When she'd had enough, she thanked Carol.

"You didn't need to stay the night. Nurse's job." Her voice was clear now, quiet, slow because of the morphine.

"I wouldn't have it any other way. I got nothing better to do." Carol put the ice bucket on the wheeled table by the wall, then came back and sat on the bed.

"They took my breast."

"I know, hon." Carol took Willa's hand.

"Knew they might have to. I don't want another surgery. Guess I'll just have one boob now."

"You don't have to decide right now. Right now, you just get better and we'll figure that out later."

"Okay." She pulled Carol's hand to her chest, her good side. Her eyes closed. "Can't move my left arm."

"They said the arm muscles are connected to your chest, so they'll be weak for a while."

"That's right. I remember now."

"You just get better," Carol whispered, her arm stretched out oddly, her back crooked, but not willing to move and disturb Willa.

Willa dozed, then gasped and jerked her hand away, looked at Carol in amazement. "Was I sleeping?"

"I think so. Morphine really does a number on you." Carol shifted to a more comfortable position and smoothed Willa's hair.

"Did JP take Linda home?" Willa's ex-husband tended to

show up to family occasions, birthday parties, and hospital waiting rooms, lurking near the edges with a long face.

"No, your Mom took Linda to your house and is staying with her tonight, like you wanted. JP's taking her back to school tomorrow. They'll come by here on their way out of town."

"Oh, yeah. I forgot. I really like morphine." She smiled crookedly at Carol, lips together.

"I'm glad you're enjoying it."

"You're a good friend, Carol. Best friend. Glad you're here."

"Wouldn't miss it. We've got to get you better fast. I've got nobody to go to the movies with while you're in here."

"You could go with Verl."

Carol shook her head. "He's not as much fun as you."

"Nobody is."

"That's for sure. You know, while we're on the subject, I need you to get better." Willa's eyes closed. "Are you awake?"

"I'm awake." Her eyes opened.

"When you were in surgery, I realized something."

"What's that." Her eyes were still open, glassy but alert.

"Well, I want to grow old with you. When we got your diagnosis, I was real scared, and the more I thought about it, the more I realized, it's you I'm looking forward to growing old with."

Willa sighed. "Because I don't have a husband to grow old with."

"Not just because of that. I want to go hiking in Palo Duro Canyon with you. Go out for Tex Mex on Fridays. We should go to New York City and see a Broadway show."

"Is *Sweeney Todd* still playing?"

"I think so. It's just that," Carol wanted to say what she'd been thinking, now that Willa was awake. "It's just that you're my best friend and I like doing things with you and we know everything about each other and we've been through a lot together."

"Like JP. You were there for me with JP."

"Yes. And I—"

"You stuck by me through that. When people said I should give him another chance, but I was just sick of it, and you told me to go ahead and throw him out."

"Well, you didn't really have to throw him out, he was gone already."

"I know, but everybody said I should take him back. But who knew where he'd been or what he'd been up to, and you were the only one who knew about all that." Willa's eyes closed.

Carol remembered well, JP's long vague business trips, his late nights, his forgetfulness. She remembered sitting with Willa on the patio after Linda had gone to sleep, eating ice cream out of the carton and drinking wine and listening to Willa speak in a low voice of her frustrations and worries, afraid to wake Linda up. Afraid of raising Linda alone. Afraid of everything.

"So, anyway," Carol shifted on the edge of the bed, trying to face Willa without pulling the covers. Willa's eyes opened. "I just wanted to say you have to get better because you're my long-term plan. All our kids are in college now, we can think about ourselves for a change."

Willa squirmed herself to the far side of the bed, against the bedrail, still on her back, her left arm limp on her stomach.

Carol stood up, confused, but Willa lifted the covers and said, "Come on in."

Carol stepped out of her shoes, pushed them under the bed, and got in beside Willa. She lay on her side, facing her friend, the blanket covering both of them, Willa's heartbeat monitor throwing a pulsing light over the room.

Willa's voice was a little slurred with the morphine. "What about Verl? He's good."

"Yeah, he's fine, but he doesn't want to hike Palo Duro Canyon with me. And he'd die before he'd go to New York City."

"True. But he's better than JP."

"Most everybody's better than JP. I'm not getting rid of him, I'm just saying I was planning on spending my time with you."

"He's only got a few more years at Hexcel. Then he can retire. Maybe he'd go places then."

"Doubt it."

"You'd miss him if he was gone." Willa turned her face toward Carol. "What would you do if Verl died?"

Carol furrowed her eyebrows, then lifted them. "I'd sell his truck."

Willa snorted. "Ow. Don't make me laugh." She took Carol's hand, brought it up to her lips, kissed it. They lay together, sleeping, not thinking about chemo or reconstruction or surgery or survival rates.

There would be time for that later.

Third Place
The White Swan
Marina Brown — Tallahassee, Florida

The forest at night is like treading inside a womb, thought Quy. This is how it is before we are born, warm, dripping, dark.

And yet, as her rubber sandals softly compressed the leaves, Quy knew that this was not a place of life. This was where spirits lingered far from home, where souls yearned to flee to a proper burial house, far from the crunch of bones and burst of bombs.

Quy walked quietly, her black hair tied tightly against the pull of vines and thorns. She no longer wore the conical hat of her village, but a bush hat now, pulled low on her face, hiding her eyes, making her anonymous in the forest, a thin, wet spirit herself.

The Central Highlands of Vietnam had been bled of its young. Fighting the French, toiling for the Vietminh and now sent south as Viet Cong guerrillas, generations of tough, wiry men and delicate girls were, like Quy, purveyors of an endless war.

But tonight—perhaps all of that would change. She inhaled the sweet composting fragrance of the forest, wondering if when she left this place that scent would remain.

As she walked, Quy imagined how the narrator of one of the VC propaganda films would explain the strange existence she now led: "Deep in the tunnel complex of Cu Chi, the vast warren of ant-like passages sheltering hundreds of guerrillas, sixteen-year-old Quy nurses the sick, feeds the living, and makes bombs to kill Americans. Day disguises itself as night within the tunnels; while night is meant for a VC to turn himself into a snake or a tiger, prowl the forests and trap his prey."

For the last month, Quy had rarely gone out of the tunnels. Bent at the waist, she, and scores of other peasant girls, scrambled through the earthen corridors, dragged sacks of rice and metal, and like insects, carried away the dead. Above, the American jets had seemed angrier. When the VC fought with bamboo sticks, the Americans threw fire; it seemed even the shaman could no longer make you invisible.

But only a few hours ago, with a boy's quickly whispered words, the twisting corridors had seemed to fill with a remembered scent of a blooming yellow apricot. Was it the sunshine she yearned for? The scent of blossoms in her hair? Perhaps escape smelled like flowers.

Quy settled her back against a tree while she waited; and as always when she was very quiet, images from the long-ago day on the hilltop came rolling back; the day she learned why she had been born—the day the puppies got away.

*

It was barely morning—before she and her father took the little dogs to market, when six-year-old Quy felt the swan. Felt it before she saw it. A cool shadow passed across her face, and she pulled wider the slit in the woven wall of her hut.

Suddenly the light changed, as if the rush of a wing were scattering drops of sun across the forest's floor. Then the swan appeared. Its arcing wings embraced a current, each feather interlocked, long neck pointed south. Like an ivory arrow, the snow-white swan was going home. The little girl looked at her own skin, white-smooth like the beautiful bird's, she thought. So different from her mother's. She had seen men smoking cigars, and the brown, rough, parchment cover of those stinking sticks made her think of her mother's hands. Ten wrinkled cigars rolling dough and making morning pancakes.

Abruptly, the sleepy image of her mother squatting over the fire, weathered brown face squinting in concentration, was brought to life when she called Quy to breakfast. "I am an unworthy daughter," Quy said out loud, as she jumped to her feet and ran to gather water for her father's tea. But she lingered too long at the water urn. Was it her fault her little white fingers reminded her of albino fish playing in iridescent circles, or that they could splash the water into rainbows that hovered in the air like colored dew.

"Quy!" The girl jumped to her feet, scattering fanciful fish into the dirt. Her father's wispy beard and small muscular frame were still imposing as he stood over her. She examined him, looking closely for signs of displeasure, but instead he smiled and handed her one of the puppies. "Gather the others into the basket. We must go. Mothers will be shopping for the tastiest puppies even now," he said.

Quy rode atop the water buffalo. Swaying gently, the smooth black skin of the buffalo's back smelled like mushrooms, and Quy rubbed her nose against the rhythmic hump.

The puppies tittered and rearranged themselves over and over in the woven panniers draped across the buffalo's rump. The fact that they would be eaten didn't disturb her; even this buffalo might one day be sacrificed with spears and an ax to honor ancestors. These puppies would be honoring someone's stomach today.

The market was filled with noise by the time they arrived. Quy's father positioned her on a tiny mat with the baskets of dogs in front of her; he would return after examining a hoe he needed to buy. She was to demand ten francs of a Vietnamese and twenty francs if a Frenchman wanted to buy a puppy for a pet. Quy nodded and placed one of her mother's large, woven conical hats on her head, feeling very proud to be left in charge.

But no sooner had her father disappeared in the warren of stalls, than an ear-splitting sputter brought shouts in Quy's direction. With a final eruption, a shiny car, so large it seemed one of its red-lacquered fenders could swallow Quy whole, came abruptly to a stop before her. As the occupants of the rolling palace began to step out, the shoppers surged forward.

A Frenchman stepped from behind the wheel. He had a thick beard and a fat red mouth that was shouting in anger. He was clearly furious at something. In any case, after conferring with an official from the market, she saw him set off into the crowd, arms waving and his face growing a deep purple.

But there was someone else in the car. It was her leg that Quy would remember. Even years later in the forests with bombs crashing above her, the vision of the French concubine's leg would always linger as it had at that moment. Purest white, as if the leg had been carved from ivory. Quy could see it was covered in silk, precious and untouchable. The child looked on and the woman stepped languidly onto the running board. The leg had only introduced her. Then came her pale arms, her milky neck, and against the creamy hue of her face, two little red lips that reminded Quy of coffee berries.

The woman held a tiny handbag and a small book. She looked around, tossing a curved helmet of golden hair. Quy heard her sigh. Quy felt sorry for the magical creature, but even more, she wanted to touch her. She wanted to know if her fingers too, were like albino fish. She wanted to run her own little hand along the arm of the woman—and she guessed it would be like touching a swan.

At that moment, a foot in the crowd kicked over the basket of puppies. Suddenly four little dogs were skittering into a labyrinth of legs. Quy cried out, people lunged for the fat little bodies, and the concubine involuntarily stepped back as shouts pointed the direction of the escape. Quy ran, distraught, laughing and on the heels of the quickest dog when suddenly it leapt forward. As Quy fell onto her knees, she heard a startled, "Oh!" Looking up, she realized the puppy had jumped into the lap of the concubine, and Quy stared into the face of a surprised, giggling woman who seemed not an ivory statue, but a kind lady of blushing flesh and gentle manner.

The woman petted the little maverick for a moment, and then her attention settled on Quy. While the swan's morning passing had blocked the sun's rays, the concubine's gaze seemed to radiate warmth.

"But you are beautiful!" the woman said to Quy, who knew a smattering of French. "You do not resemble the others here. What is your name, child?"

Quy could barely speak, but she whispered her name as the concubine reached out her pale hand and cupped Quy's face.

"Look, my cherie," and the woman pulled Quy's little arm against her own, "You are as pale as I am! Perhaps we are sisters!" she laughed. Handing the puppy to someone nearby, the concubine took a writing pen from her handbag and began to write something in her book. When she was finished, she handed it to Quy. "This is a promise, my little Quy. Don't forget." Quy took the book and was handed the puppy—and then its captured brothers all replaced in their baskets.

When she turned back, the car was restarting, the bearded man still shouting behind the wheel. Soon only the receding profile of the concubine as it turned into silhouette was left.

The practical marketplace, however, had lost itself in novelty for only a time. Now the chickens were cackling and the pigs were grunting and all would resume as it had always been.

However, one old man, perhaps a teacher, squatted beside her and asked to see the book. He smiled as he read the French words aloud to Quy. "One day, come south to Saigon, ma Cherie. You will be greatly admired for your beauty. A pale little swan like you will indeed find great success."

The old man gently touched her arm and nodded in agreement. "Protect your beauty from the sun," he said. "Protect it from the wishes of men. And one day, as the woman has written—in Saigon the world will become yours."

Quy didn't understand everything, but in that moment, she felt that a purpose had been laid before her. And that night as she dreamed, swans and albino fish played happily together in the warm waters of the Mekong far away to the South.

*

Somewhere in the distance, a bomb fell. A bomb did not fall alone, Quy knew. Others would follow. In Cu Chi's dark warren, the tunnels trembled as if responding to the pain of the earth far away.

Quy looked at the slim young man squatting beside her, his black pajamas stained and wet in the candle's light. Minh rarely whispered. But he was whispering now, so close that Quy felt his breath tickle her ear. A teen-ager like Quy, Minh was a painter. On other nights, he'd told her of red powders he could turn into sunsets and green dust his brush could make into leaves so real they would blow in the wind. Quy knew that with their VC comrades, Minh pounded American tank parts into land mines, armed camouflaged pits with nails and wires, and sometimes even shared his blood with wounded cadre through chicken veins and scavenged electrical cords.

Yet, this thin man was not like them. Scratching at the earth with a stick, Minh could make rabbits and mountains and images of wild deer spring up from the dirt. And when she told him of the book she carried in her pocket, he had said only, "Yes, yes." And then his eyes looked very far away, toward the south. And she remembered he had let his fingers shyly touch hers.

Now Minh's words spilled out. In the dim light, his eyes were wide as he told her quickly that the dream they both had dreamt separately was about to become real. "We shall go tonight, Quy. You will leave first—I will join you one hour later."

It was hot in the tunnel, the air outside turning to steam. Perspiration made their skin glow in the thin light, and for a moment, Minh imagined the translucent skin of the girl beside him had turned to alabaster. Perhaps one day he would sculpt her, he thought—far away from this place. His hand touched hers. They were chaste, these two. Believers in beauty; it was the only aphrodisiac they permitted themselves.

Quy had guessed that he was planning their escape. They would surely be shot if found out. But Minh had described the large Americans as kind to those carrying white scarves. And they would be allowed to go to Saigon, he'd said, to safety, to the lake with softly-rowed boats—where maybe even love could grow. And she agreed with a slight nod of her head. The concubine had foretold her future. "We will fly like birds, to the south."

Quy had been waiting for nearly one hour in a hesitant rain just under the rise that was the patrol perimeter of the American base.

Her eyes closed from time to time as she squatted on one wet haunch and then the other, listening to the sounds of the forest, awake with closed eyes or at moments, asleep with eyes open. And then Minh was beside her. Again he was whispering, but this time, his words came in a rush. The Americans were planning something bad tonight. Something dangerous was about to happen. They must hurry back to the tunnels; not even a white scarf would protect them.

"Hurry, little swan, hurry," he pleaded. She took his hand and then the bombing began. The explosions didn't come first. Nor the whine of plummeting metal ripping through the trees. It was the shudder of earth, wave-like spasms violating the forest floor and rising up Quy's legs. Then came the sudden evacuation of air and sound, as if the whole sensory world were being swallowed. Quy took two steps. She saw herself running—but it was a dream.

The bomb burst open beside them. A radiance that enveloped everything, destroyed everything, illuminated the two tiny figures. Minh turned to look at Quy. Her eyes, round as sequins, glittered in the napalm's dance and the whiteness of her face reflected the rupturing trees and burning clouds. Even their breath seemed on fire.

In a thunder of white phosphorus, her hand evaporated and his eyes. The second bomb ate out the forest. Again and again, explosions filled the air. And then a third bomb erupted above their heads. Quy's black hair curled to powder. In a tornado of fire and greasy phosphorous, Minh's fingernails softened and slowly dripped to the forest floor.

The planes passed again and again in their hour of predawn exercise until at last, worn-out and empty, they grew tired of the game. The dawn raid gave way to an azure morning. The pilots departed, feeling hungry for breakfast.

The forest continued to erupt with exploding shrapnel and bursting trees, but slowly, it too subsided in a kind of sob. Pushing aside burning leaves and hot soil, the hidden cadre now crawled out of their maze to gaze at the forest. Seared and crackling, the canopy's blackened stumps jabbed helplessly at the sky. The soldiers walked about in silence, slapping at embers thrown up by their rubber sandals. There could be nothing living here, no one to repair with tape or wire or suture. Only a tiny movement in a crater drew their attention—perhaps just a shift of wind.

Impossibly, it was a hand that moved. It slowly stroked the dead animal beside it, an animal without skin, roasted red and wet.

"You will be my eyes, beautiful Quy." came a broken voice. "Though I will not see you, your pale skin, like moonlight on a swan, will light my days." There was a pause and the cadre expected no more.

And then more softly, "Soon we will fly to Saigon, to float on the lake, you beneath your parasol for all the city to admire." Flesh rolled in tiny scrolls about the man's face and chest. Where there were eyes, dark emptiness ran deep and red. Minh coughed; a hot, stinging cinder scraped at his throat. He held her wrist, imagining the soft white skin of her body that would one day wrap him like satin and soothe his blindness.

Imperceptibly, a breeze began to grow. Fallen cinders stirred on the forest floor. As if from a sigh, cool currents began to thread between the blackened trees.

And then it began. The stricken cadre looked up at what seemed to be transparent bits of rice paper, white, powdery, drifting in the air, falling along their arms and in their hair, as white as the skin of a swan—incandescent in flight, the spirals eddied down in good-bye. The pieces of flesh hovered in a tiny whirlwind over the darkened form of Minh until at last, the breeze freshening toward the South, the fragments rose—a promise to be kept on a bright day in May.

Adult Novel Excerpt

Judge – Ginger Marks
Clearwater, Florida

First Place
Sisters in Exile
Betty Cotter — Shannock, Rhode Island

Chapter 1
July 5, 1946

Alice came into the pantry looking for her sister, who was snipping tea roses. Meredith was needed upstairs.

"She won't have anyone else. It's all the buttons, and you know how she hates to be touched."

Despite all the post-war shortages, with dozens of weddings a month, somehow their baby sister, Lenore, had found a ready-made gown. When Meredith arrived home it had mocked her, a ghostly bride on Mother's dress form.

Upstairs she found Lenore with her back to the bedroom door, flailing her arms. They'd only gotten five buttons fastened, and the dress must have had fifty. Meredith took a deep breath.

"Please be quick about it," Lenore said.

It was a close day, rainy and humid. Someone had cracked a window, and water rattled down the gutters. Despite the heat, goosebumps dimpled Lenore's back. Meredith gathered the folds and did the best she could to avoid touching her sister. In Lenore's difficult childhood, a bunched-up sock or scratchy slip could send her into hysterics. Now she held herself as still as that mannequin in the corner, as though she could squirm away from the dress entirely.

Six, seven, eight. The material, stiffer than expected, resisted Meredith's efforts, and the buttonholes felt small. When Alice got married, Mother had sewn a zipper into the side of her gown and camouflaged it cleverly with a pleat. She was good at hiding things.

"Is Cal here yet?"

Meredith swallowed. Nine. Ten. "No," she managed. When he did arrive, she could only hope to be tied up somehow, either still wrestling with the gown, or finishing the bouquets.

"For heaven's sake, what's taking you so long?"

Twelve, thirteen, fourteen. In her haste Meredith grazed her sister's backbone with a nail. Lenore jumped like a nervous horse. What would she do when Cal put his broad, rough hands around her waist? When he drew down the zipper of her nightgown? Meredith clamped her teeth. Seventeen. For the age she'd been. Eighteen. Nineteen. Twenty. For the lonely years that followed.

Mother poked her head in the door. "How are you coming? Cal and his brother are here."

"Oh." Lenore shuddered and looked over her shoulder. "Come *on*."

"Where are the corsages?" Mother leaned farther in but kept her feet in the hall.

"On the counter. I got interrupted."

"You still have to comb out my hair," Lenore said. She'd had a permanent yesterday and set it in pin curls last night.

Mother disappeared again. Twenty-five. Twenty-six. Of course, Ned would be the best man. Meredith had forgotten about Cal's family. His mother, Edie. His brother, Ned. What could she say to them, after all these years?

"You're pinching me."

Meredith breathed deeply and relaxed her grip on the fabric. How could Lenore have gained weight just since the last fitting, on Wednesday? With effort, she cinched the waist and continued northward. Twenty-eight. Twenty-nine. Thirty. So the years would continue, interminable and solitary, until the end.

***

Alice peeked from the den into the living room, where four rows of chairs had been laid out. The gathering was small. Cal had invited his mother; brother Ned and his wife Cora, and their half-sister, Diane Richmond. With Alice's husband, Jim, and their two girls, Lenore had only seven guests—well, eight, Alice thought, laying a hand on the ridge where her belly swelled beneath her organza matron of honor dress.

Alice watched as Merry bent her dark head toward her nieces. Merry should be the bride. Everything about this impromptu ceremony seemed unfair—the rush to put it together; Merry's hasty trip home, her canceled summer research; and now her seat in the audience, where she would have to watch their baby sister marry Cal Austin, of all people.

Finally Lenore appeared in the shadowy den, her father holding her by a shaky arm. At the piano, cousin Ruth Annie Day plinked a few notes before finding the right key. Fair or not, there was no turning back now.

Reverend Montgomery began in his droning way. Meredith faced forward, focusing on a spot of wallpaper beyond Lenore's head. A "long-distance love," Mother had called it. What could they know about each other from writing letters?

And what had they shared, in the few months since his discharge? Had Cal held a buttercup under her chin? Run with her down the beach? Had Lenore touched the throbbing vein in his neck, or felt his muscular arms circling her?

"What therefore God hath joined together, let no man tear asunder," the minister said.

Of course they had shared all that, and probably more. Meredith took Ellen's tiny right hand and cupped it in both of hers as one might a moth you were trying to keep alive.

The minister asked for the ring. Ned produced it from his breast pocket and passed it to Cal. He took it in his left hand, regarded it for a beat, then looked out toward the family. His gaze did not find Meredith — the looking outward was general, sweeping, and confused. Then — and Merry was sure she saw this — he shook his head (to clear it? to cast away doubt?) and turned back toward the woman who was about to become his wife.

After the ceremony, Lenore and Cal drifted to the back of the living room. I'm a married woman, Lenore kept saying to herself, a married woman. She waited for some transformation to take place, but she felt as awkward and out of place as she always did. It didn't help that Cal stood a few inches away without touching her, and that no one seemed to know what to do. None of Cal's family got along. Maybe this was why everyone clumped together, not saying much. Lenore tugged on the sleeve of Cal's Army uniform, but when he turned toward her she didn't know what to say. He gave her a quick smile and squeezed her hand, his wedding ring clanking against hers. *My husband!* She would have said it out loud, but something stopped her.

Where was Merry? She could always calm her down. But Merry was nowhere to be seen. The more Lenore looked around the living room, the more panicked she felt. The buttons that had taken so long to fasten cut into her flesh. If she didn't spot Merry soon she might faint, or be sick—what a way to embarrass herself on the most important day of her life.

"Oh, she's in the kitchen," Mother said off-handedly, but when Lenore slipped into the next room, Meredith wasn't there.

***

Merry was in the mudroom with their father, who was slicing watermelon on the hardwood counter. She had brought out a platter and took each red slice as it fell from his knife.

"You be careful on that mountain," he said, without preamble.

"Yes, Daddy." She had done wildflower research in the Great Smokies before, but never had she camped out.

"Don't take any chances." His knife slipped through the rind. "She wanted you to stand up for her, you know. Of course she had no idea what she was asking. I put a stop to it."

Merry took a slimy slice and moved it down the platter. "Thank you."

"In my day, a man had a certain honor."

This would not do. "Daddy, don't."

"I'm glad you came home, Merry, but I'm not sure I would have in your shoes. I told your mother to leave it be. But she seems to be under the impression you need to face this squarely. Feels to me more like rubbing it in."

The chunk, chunk, chunk of watermelon cutting continued. Slices ringed the platter. With each slash, the knife released more aroma, and with it months of soil-tending, weeding, and watering. Daddy had always fed them well—potatoes and squash for the root cellar, eggs and milk, apples and pears from his orchard. But you could not take for granted the first watermelon. He might as well throw his heart onto the sideboard and quarter it.

"What I can't get over," he said, blade poised above the melon's hind end, "is how he's taken my daughter away from me, again."

She told him not to worry, that Lenore was only moving down the road, for heaven's sake. And then he looked at her dead-on.

"I wasn't talking about Lenore. I was talking about you. I'm afraid you'll never come home again."

Lenore did not want to eat. Nothing on the dining room table interested her—not the mounds of potato salad, the cold sliced ham, or the deviled eggs with caps of shiny yellow. In fact, all of it turned her stomach, though she usually felt nauseous only in the morning. Even the three tiers of wedding cake, with their bullets of silver sugar, radiated a cloying sweetness. Somehow she would have to tell Cal not to shove it into her mouth.

Everyone crushed around the table, pushing her forward, refusing to take their share until her plate was full. So she picked off a few stalks of celery and a scoop of chicken salad. She would just walk around with the plate for a while until she could stash it somewhere. As a child she would hide whatever embarrassed her—a bloody handkerchief, a ruined sewing project, a ripped homework paper. Her mother eventually found these discarded remnants but rarely if ever confronted her about them.

Cal had disappeared. Balancing the plate, Lenore moved into the living room, past his brother Ned's wife and then her two nieces, hoping no one would talk to her. There he was, in the doorway to the hall, with Meredith. *Her husband.*

"I can't," Meredith was saying.

"Can't what?" Lenore sidled up to them. She waited for Cal to smile. When he smiled it was almost as good as Meredith for easing her jitters.

"Can't talk," Merry said. "I mean, I've things to do."

Lenore wondered what that might be. Had she been a difficult bride? Had she expected her sisters to do too much? "You never came through the receiving line," she said. "I wanted to thank you."

"I was helping with the food." Meredith looked like she wanted to run, not walk, away from them both. Had Cal said something wrong? But no. He didn't look upset.

"You don't have to thank me," Merry added. "I just wanted the table to look nice."

"Not that." Hadn't their mother set the table? "She helped me get into my gown," Lenore told Cal. "Look at these buttons."

"Beautiful," he said, as she twirled. "Beautiful," he repeated, his voice fading.

"You should eat," Meredith said, motioning to the plate. Lenore had forgotten it and thought with dismay that it would now be much more difficult to jettison.

"That's not much," Cal said. "Let me get you a real dish, Len."

"I don't know. Maybe I should change first." Yes. She would go upstairs, get out of this straight-jacket, put on her going-away suit. That would take time. They would all forget about dinner, maybe even the cake.

"I was just going upstairs," Meredith said. She seemed pleased. *Finally*, Lenore thought, *I have said the right thing.*

"What time is it?"

Consulting his watch, Cal reported it was a quarter to three.

Lenore turned to him. "It's been perfect, hasn't it?" Suddenly it became vital that he agree with her. He had said nothing of consequence to her since "I do."

"It's not over yet." His voice was light and teasing. What did that mean? Was he happy? But he added only, "Let me get you some real food."

"No, no, no. I'm going up with Merry."

"All right, then." He gave her arm a little squeeze, took away the plate, and then was gone.

***

Upstairs, Alice laid out the going-away dress on one of the beds. She pressed her hands against the forest green rayon, smoothing out the folds, while Merry stood behind Lenore, trying to get her buttons undone. This was what Alice missed, living in Florida. The three of them in this tiny room. Three sisters, together, at home, where nothing could come between them. "This is the last time we'll be together like this," she said.

The truth was they had not lived as a family for a long time, yet this wedding, more than her own, more than Meredith's moving down South, seemed to mark the end of something.

"But you'll come home, won't you?" Lenore's voice, muffled as Meredith tugged her dress over her head, held a trace of panic.

God, she hoped so. "Of course. The girls will be here in the summers, and someday your children. It's just getting passed to a new generation, is all."

"Yes, your children," Merry said, her voice wistful.

"And we won't be in Florida forever," Alice added decisively. "I can tell you that."

***

Cal passed a sliver of cake into Lenore's waiting mouth, and she bit off what she could. Snap, snap, snap, Meredith shot pictures with her Brownie camera. She was always taking pictures.

"What about a family portrait?" demanded cousin Ruth Annie, after Lenore had swallowed the dry slice with difficulty. "All of you together. You just show me what button to push and where to look through."

Ruth Annie herded them into the living room and made a great show of moving everyone around. Lenore felt the room spin. It had grown so humid she could hardly breathe.

Everyone pressed in. Lenore's arm smushed into Cal's shoulder. On his other side was Meredith. Ruth Annie pronounced herself satisfied and ordered them all to say "cheese."

After that things happened quickly. Meredith thought, *It's almost over, thank God.* Alice told her husband to bring down Lenore's suitcase, and while Cal and Lenore huddled at the breakfront, opening envelopes, Alice jotted down who had given what and Cal folded the bills into his wallet. They left unopened the pyramid of boxes. Edie sniffled into her handkerchief. Ruth Annie began playing "Oh Susannah," while the party hung around the dining room. Goodbyes, once begun, became protracted, and Meredith saw Cal looking at his watch.

He was steering Lenore gently toward the back door when Darcy stepped in front of them. "Where's the bouquet? Aren't you going to throw your bouquet?"

"Oh, heavens, I forgot all about it." Lenore looked around. "Where's Merry? Oh, there you are. What did you do with my flowers?"

Meredith dashed upstairs. She had put Lenore's and Alice's bouquets on the bedroom windowsill, and now their petals bubbled with rain. They felt heavier than before, almost too weighty to lift. Maybe Lenore could hand one to each of the girls, and then it would be over.

But Darcy and Ellen demanded a bouquet toss. They all moved into the front hall. Meredith hung back, near the console Emerson radio, where Diane leaned against the wall, lighting a cigarette.

"I was just thinking," Diane said, her voice low, "of that day the three of us went to the quarry."

"Don't," was all Meredith could say, even though no one else had heard. Of course, Diane remembered all of it. Cal's sister had been—what? Nine years old? And determined to tag along.

"Come now, girls, don't be bashful," Ruth Annie was saying.

"I bet you never thought it would turn out like this," Diane said, whispering in her husky voice. "You must have been some surprised."

Lenore climbed halfway up the stairs, as high as she could go without hitting the ceiling, peeked behind her and lobbed the roses. They landed on the floor at Meredith's feet, lying there like a funeral spray on a grave. Meredith took one step back.

Darcy reached the booty before Ellen. Some unladylike scuffling ensued. Finally Alice declared that Darcy should get the bride's bouquet and Ellen could have her mother's. Ellen eyed the consolation prize warily, but, seeing Darcy's abrupt shift of gaze, realized she might have gotten the better end of the bargain. The girls began parading about. If only roses would be the only thing they would fight over, Meredith thought, forever and ever, amen.

She turned to find Cal watching her. Had he heard Diane? Was it possible he, too, had imagined a different sort of outcome? Or did he just feel sorry for her? Well, she would not be pitied, not by Ruth Annie Day or Diane Richmond or her mother or father, and certainly not by her new brother-in-law.

He stood in her path now, blocking her way.

"Excuse me." She could see it all. His long, deep dive into the water. His head surfacing. The rivulets that ran down his back when he climbed onto the granite rocks.

He seemed about to speak, but then the guests moved, en masse, pushing them all toward the kitchen door.

Jim dashed into the rain to load Alice's suitcase into the Chevy. They all clumped together under the lean-to with cups of rice and began pelting Lenore and Cal with kernels.

Everyone began shouting and waving, but Merry turned on her heel, heading up the back stairs to the sisters' old bedroom. Back on its dress form, Lenore's wedding gown glowed like a weak lamp. Its left sleeve brushed her arm as she scooted onto the window seat. She looked down to see the Chevy roll slowly by, to the end of the driveway, where it stopped. For a moment its brake lights glowed red. Then the car turned left and pulled away, toward the north, past the elms in the front yard and out of sight.

Second Place
Wildwind
Lauren Strach — Yachats, Oregon

Chapter 1

"I've confirmed the U-Haul for next week," Sonny said as he divided eggs and pancakes onto three breakfast plates. Birdie's was the one with the Mickey Mouse-shaped pancakes. The added scrambled eggs gave Mickey a halo of soft yellow hair.

"Perfect. I got the van hitch installed yesterday," I said. One more thing checked off the list. It was early December, and we were packing for our cross-country move from Ann Arbor, Michigan to the coast of Oregon. We'd be there before Christmas. We were heading to Wildwind, Sonny's recently inherited family home. I'd always been a rolling stone, chasing education, internships, doctoral fellowships, experiences, but now, finally, I was ready to put down roots for our family.

"Birdie, come and eat," I said. "You can finish your drawing after school." Our four-year-old daughter had been busy creating yet another gift since she woke up.

"I called Helena and told her we'd be there by Christmas Eve. Birdie will wake up in our new home on Christmas morning," Sonny said. "Helena's so excited. It's been too long since there was a child for Santa to visit." Helena, the local librarian, was the caretaker of the house, of Sonny's late great aunt Edith, and of all things Wildwind. It seemed we inherited her along with the house.

All the pieces were falling into place. Today was Sonny's final chemo session. Then we had to wait one more week for his last bloodwork review. Piled in the garage were labeled boxes of our essential things. Those would go with us in the U-Haul. The rest of our belongings were heading for storage. We'd spend the winter semester in Oregon. We hadn't made any plans after that. For now, it was enough to take time off. Make memories with Birdie. Let Sonny heal. Allow the stress to flow out of my body. My hand went to my belly. Two embryos were waiting at the fertility clinic. Maybe in the summer, we could try again. I smiled at the thought of twins. Birdie would love that.

"Okay," Birdie agreed, "but don't look at my picture. It's a surprise."

"I would never peek," I agreed. "Put it in your special box, and we won't open it until Christmas."

Birdie grinned as she climbed onto her chair, sensing our excitement for this next adventure. We were lucky to have one.

"Are you sure you feel up to driving?" I asked Sonny one more time as I got ready to leave. "Sarah can pick up Birdie from preschool for the playdate. And she could give you a ride to chemo."

"Yes, I'm sure, Miss Worrier. I may have only one arm, but it's in fine working condition. And I want to see Birdie before chemo. You wouldn't want me to miss that, would you?"

I was increasingly nervous about Sonny driving on snowy, icy Michigan roads. Who knew what the cumulative effects of the chemo were? I was a worrier. He was a doctor, and he knew his body. I had to trust him. But still. I wanted to insist he stop driving until he was healthy again, but it wasn't my place.

"Okay. If you're sure." I pushed away my misgivings. Sonny would never put his child at risk.

"Have a great lecture today," he said, kissing me goodbye. I was heading to Detroit to speak to the League of Women

Voters, my final speaking engagement before the move.

"Birdie, come on, climb in your car seat," I said. It took a few extra minutes, but we built in time to honor her attempts at autonomy.

"I love you," Sonny said.

"I love you, too. We'll celebrate your chemo graduation tonight. Onward to Oregon."

"Onward," Birdie's lilting voice echoed from the back. Sonny finished buckling her in and kissed her. Her little arms went around his neck.

"Love you, Daddy."

"Love you, too, my little bird."

Despite the falling snow and slick roads, the drive back from Detroit was quicker than I'd expected. I hummed along with the radio as I thought about the question-and-answer session. It'd been illuminating, as always.

I'd written a book, *Women's Voices*, that tapped into the zeitgeist of the moment. It reflected who I was, had been, and was becoming. It included what I'd learned and what I taught. I'd written it for my grandmother, my mother, my daughter, and for mixed-race women like myself. "Use your insights. Make a difference," Sonny always said. And I tried.

Women's studies departments and book clubs had adopted my book. It had triggered conversations awakening on the edges of our culture. Sonny had been right. I needed to let my experiences serve a purpose.

I took the hospital elevator to the fourth-floor Oncology clinic. I was early for Sonny's session, which was unusual for me. I was usually the one dawdling or caught running behind schedule. Wouldn't Sonny be surprised when he got here?

I hadn't taught this semester; I'd used it for speaking engagements and researching my next book. Sonny hadn't taken the semester off. He'd continued with his medical school administrative role, ignoring the toll of the chemotherapy.

"Hi Janet," I said, checking in with the Oncology Unit admin. "I'm early, but I'll get settled before Sonny arrives." I dropped my bag near our usual chairs. Patient chair, partner chair. When had a cancer regimen become 'usual'? Like it was normal to sit with your beloved while poison drips through the port in his chest? Seemed like a bastardization of those words.

"Sounds good," she replied. "Snacks in the fridge. Tea and coffee are hot. Happy holidays."

It was all so very civilized. Because polite society frowned upon the ranting and raving and the tearing of clothes.

"Hiya, Sarah, hey Judy," I called out to the women sitting next to our chairs. Both of them taught at the school of nursing. They were part of our bi-weekly Wednesday afternoon gang. Judy had breast cancer, her second round, this time it had spread to her lymph nodes. They knew the chemo routine and had taken us under their wings. Sarah had shaved her head in solidarity, and they wore pink crocheted pussy hats over their bald heads. Today their hand-stitched 'F**k Cancer' shirts were neon chartreuse.

I waved at Ken, a retired doc, and his daughter. He'd been the beloved doctor to the other doctors, and here he was. Physician heal thyself. If only.

And across from us was Aria, an artist. She had a rotating crew of old boyfriends who sat with her. Maybe someday we'd meet for coffee when chemo was over, and I'd have the nerve to ask for a flow chart of how they all fit together.

This was Ann Arbor, throw a stone, hit an academic/medical professional/artist. And here we were, lined up like Chaucer's archetypes, representing a cross-section of our town. Tinker/tailor/soldier/spy. Butcher/baker/candlestick maker.

I called our merry band of Wednesday chemo warriors the Good Luck Club. Because as long as we were walking this road, we were lucky to have each other. I'd learned that perspective from my husband.

Before I'd met Sonny, after the accident that derailed my ballet career, and during the stress of graduate school, I admit, I could get blue. Okay, I guess that isn't accurate. Depression. It dogged my heels. Sonny was the lion-tamer when it came to chasing away any pessimism. No darkness allowed. Not even with this cancer thing. Especially with this cancer thing.

"Your name is perfect," I said to him in those early days when we were getting to know each other. "Except..."

"What do you mean, except?" he asked, pulling me closer as we lay on the couch reading sections of the newspaper, passing them back and forth like an old married couple.

"It's misspelled. It should be Sunny. Because that's what you bring when you enter the room."

Time had only proved how accurate that early assessment was. Despite what life threw his way, he accepted it and moved forward. No matter he'd been blown up in convoy headed for a field hospital in Iraq. Although he lost an arm, he could still teach. No matter our infertility. He knew our perfect baby was only waiting to time her entrance. No matter he got cancer from exposure to chemical warfare. Epidemiologists studying cancer rates in returning vets could use his data. He always found the silver lining.

When Birdie arrived, I had to agree with his optimism. She was the child we were waiting to meet. She had blue eyes, with a smile that never stopped, just like Sonny. She was petite like me, with a dancer's natural grace that took our breath away.

We loved watching her sleep at night. "My cancer is just a thing, a hurdle to get over," Sonny said. "At least it isn't her."

"At least it isn't her," I would whisper back, tucking in her blanket.

Sonny. Sunny. How I loved that name. Words, they were important. They held power. They reflected the soul. They were instruments that could change the world. *Birdie.* Her given name Beatrix was for Sonny's mother. Middle name, Rose. Because she was the flower of my life. My bloom, my seed. But Birdie was who she was, the name she seemed to have chosen for herself.

Where is he? Everyone seemed to be early today, as if the sooner they got hooked up and started the drip, the faster they'd be done. But not Sonny. That's odd. If ever there was a man who liked to be prompt, it was my husband.

I looked around. Every grouping of patients was an inspiration for my new book on voice and creativity. Each person had created their reality, cocooning themselves as they traversed the unthinkable. Creativity wasn't only arts and crafts and making and performing. It was also in the rituals that smoothed the road of life, that eased the bumps. *Fuck cancer.* Love those shirts. I needed to get one.

Where is he? Sonny's years as a triathlete, a soldier, and a doctor gave him unique insights into his body and what it could do. He lived life as if his chemo was an assignment. Accept the side effects, ignore the threat of his mortality. Push through, anticipate the coming joys.

Where is he? The sounds of the hospital grew louder as I waited, grating on my nerves. Sirens seemed to be screaming right around the corner. Emergencies were a way of life in this medical complex. I had to quit being so jumpy.

Where is he? The hands on the wall clock had kept their constant movement, and now Sonny was officially late. I called his cell, but it went to voice mail. *That's odd.* I called my friend, Sarah, where Sonny was going for Birdie's play date, but no answer. I could text him, but he was driving.

Where is he? I know, I could find his location on my phone.

There he is. He's right around the corner, still close to the preschool. He must be running late. Okay, I could walk over and see if he was having trouble.

"Janet, I'm going to check on Sonny. I'll be back as quick as I can."

"Okay, stay warm."

I stepped through the sliding double doors. The winter wind hit my face, making my eyes water. I tucked my head deep into my coat as I turned the corner. *Flashing lights.* I see a familiar sedan, crumpled and entwined with an oversized SUV. I start running.

How could he? *He'd promised me he wasn't compromised.*
How could I have done that speech? *I never should have left.*
How could I have let him drive our girl? *Come back to me.*
Guilt and sorrow pull from the same pot of darkness.

From a distance, I see Sonny's distorted, misshapen face splayed against the shattered window, pinned by the airbag. I run as the first responders pull the car seat from the back. Hope chokes my throat with suppressed desire. But the body of a broken doll is removed. And my screams shatter the frozen air.

Chapter 2

Funerals create a sense of purpose, of focus. Finish the photo display boards. Select the right outfit. As if completing those tasks would keep the world from coming to an end. *False.* It was all false. The world had already come to an end. It was the end. The lives of my sunny Sonny and my girl Birdie were over.

Usually, I was a fan of celebrating rites of passage. But not this. My entire body recoiled against this.

Birdie. *Gone.* She was everywhere. She was nowhere.

Sonny. *Gone.* He was everywhere. He was nowhere.

"Sarah?" I asked as she sat with me on the couch in her family room. It had been seven hours since I'd had a family.

"Yes?"

"Please just do it. Do it all."

"I will. All you have to do is show up."

"Plan the visitation and funeral on the same day. I don't think I can hold it together for two times. And do it quickly. I want it over."

"I'll take care of it."

Sarah, who put the best in best friend, stepped in with efficiency and love. Sarah organized the service and made the necessary calls. Sarah read the paperwork and told me where to sign. A former accountant is useful at times like these.

"You're moving in with us," she declared. I didn't know what else to do.

Her girls had been Birdie's best friends. I loved her girls. I hated her girls. No, no, of course not, never hate. Not jealousy, either. An unremitting ache of loss at every toy left on the floor. Mealtimes weren't a problem. I didn't eat. I took my sleeping pills and stayed in my room.

The same friends who organized the cancer treatment meal train signed up for a new kind of duty. The "keep an eye on Carolina" duty. There was a secret handing off to the next member of the relay team for each part of the day.

I lost my voice. Not literally. I could still speak if spoken to. But I had nothing to say. I was without words. I had always used words to create meaning in my world. To articulate my deepest emotions. To share my thoughts and insights. But there was a void where my words used to live. A vortex of null space. A black hole.

Flowers? Casket? Caskets? Music? Readings?

I could care less. *No. Wait.* I couldn't care less. Whichever. Whatever. Laws of grammar? No parent should bury their child. Let's start with that basic rule. If a person says, "I couldn't care less" about something, it means that the amount of care and concern they have about something could not be any less, any lower. This makes sense. Therefore, when someone says, "I could care less," it should mean the opposite, that they are concerned. So, yes, I couldn't care less.

Sonny's parents, older and frailer than they'd been at Thanksgiving, came as soon as they heard. But why? There was nothing they could do. They were burying their only child, their only grandchild. They stared at me with hollow eyes at the funeral home, eyes sunken into their faces like Halloween ghouls. I stared back at them with my own blank look.

"What can we do? What can I do?" Sonny's father asked, over and over again. He was used to being in charge, of being the capable one. Finally, I gave him a job.

"Can you call Helena at Wildwind? She's expecting us. Can you let her know?"

Let her know. That was the mandate.

My mother flew up from the Florida retirement community she had moved to when my dad died. We'd visited her there, Birdie digging in the white sands, surfing with her water wings in the ocean waves. My mother had lost her husband and survived. What lessons could I learn from her? Any? Nothing. The long valley of the shadow of death. How do I get out of there? The stages of mourning. What were they? I guess I would know soon enough. Later. When I cared.

Words. Had they ever been so empty? One more cornerstone of my life vacated.

"Oh my God, I could never handle what you are going through." *I'm not.*

"I know exactly how you feel." *I doubt it.*

"Let me know if you need anything." *All that I need is gone.*

"At least they didn't suffer." *I'm doing enough for all of us.*

"God never gives you more than you can handle." *I can't even respond to this one.*

"Stay strong." *Stay is the operative word. What is my world without them?*

At the funeral, I was the vision of Jackie Kennedy from the history books, minus the adorable children and the black mantilla. I had a role to play. I had to be the vessel for the grief of others. I needed to receive their voices, to hold their memories of Sonny and Birdie. *It's too much.* I didn't have the emotional depth to carry anything for anyone. And yet I did.

Accidents like this brought out the fears of one's mortality. I noticed the mourners holding their children a bit tighter. Make the sign of the cross. Throw salt over your shoulder. Do whatever it takes to keep this random evil from darkening your doorstep. It could happen to you. But it didn't. It happened to me.

Third Place
White Cloud Free
Peter Johnson — Naples, Florida

Prologue

I am 22 years old and it doesn't occur to me that my degree in English from New York University might not qualify me to save a fully grown cow from an angry swarm of killer bees. My buddy, Jack, on the other hand, is more reasonable about the whole endeavor.

"We have been in the Peace Corps for only two weeks," he observes. As we traipse across a pasture, his words are punctuated by the soft popping sound of bees smacking into my veil as they try to find a vulnerable patch of flesh on which to martyr themselves.

"So?" I say crossing my arms. It is the hour of the day just after sunset, when it is not yet dark. The pasture is enclosed on all sides by a lush jungle and the thigh-high chartreuse grass is dotted with reddish earthen termite mounds that, in the waning light, look vaguely like phallic spectres.

"So, I don't think we have been trained for this," he says simply, his face obscured by the veil. Jack is a giant man who was the starting offensive tackle for the 2001-2002 University of California football team. Owing to his size, he played football pretty much his whole life—and was quick to tell anyone who would listen that he hated every minute of it.

"C'mon, Jack," I implore. "You know that a situation like this won't be covered in our training. Besides, we are the only people who can do this. None of the farmers have a bee suit."

Even though I've only known Jack for a couple of weeks, I suspect that appeals to heroism or adventure won't work on him. He is the hometown hero of his small farming town in Northern California. Unlike me, he did not join the Peace Corps to be the protagonist of his own personal odyssey; but rather, he travelled halfway around the world to escape all the lofty hopes that had been foisted on him.

Before he has a chance to demur, we are interrupted by a gurgled, miserable bellow of a cow somewhere in the grass toward the far side of the pasture.

"We can't just leave her out here," I say, setting off toward the sound. Jack plods after me, every step evoking a new wave of frenzied bees glancing off of my canvas bee suit. A few land on the veil in front of my face, vainly thrusting their tiny stingers through the gossamer as if to convey a dire warning from their berserk sorority.

The cow emits a few more anguished groans before I find her lying on her side, resigned to her fate, white from the honeybee venom sacs covering her body.

"Oh God," Jack whispers as he lumbers to a spot beside me.

I take a step closer and the cow makes a half-hearted attempt to rise to its feet, wriggling against its own halter, which is attached to a lead rope that is stretched taut from a place where it is tied to a large clump of flaxen grasses. The beast collapses again with a hollow thud.

"Easy girl," I coo, brushing dozens of bees from around the creature's protuberant, wet black eye. Her enormous rib cage rises and falls with breath that is uneven and labored.

"Jack, go untie her," I say, motioning toward the place where the rope seems to be tied. A moment later the rope goes slack and Jack joins me where I am squatting over the creature's head, futilely swatting at the bees that continue to attack there.

"What now?" Jack says. "Cows weigh like 1,000 pounds."

I grab the rope out of Jack's hand and begin to pull at the creature. "C'mon girl," I say encouragingly, jerking at the rope. She rocks back and forth a couple of times, finally heaving the front half of her body upon a pair of improbably spindly legs. She pauses for a moment in this twisted position and then collapses again with a sickening thud.

I look over at Jack who shrugs his massive shoulders.

"Well we can't just leave her here to die," I say. "Take her back legs and help me drag her back toward the village."

Progress is slow and halting as we drag the corpulent bovine over broken stalks of grass. I try to ignore the awful way her massive head skids and bounces across the ground in front of me, its roving globular eye somehow unperturbed by the whole ordeal.

The bees continue their ceaseless attack, though soon I am breathing so heavily that I barely notice it.

"Hold on," I say breathlessly, dropping the legs. "I need a break." A long avenue of matted grass extends away from the massive supine creature back toward the place, still visible in the distance, where we found her.

"This is horrifying," Jack says after a few moments of silence. "Like this might be the worst thing I've ever seen."

"What I find horrifying," I say, still gasping for breath, "is how much easier this is for you than it is for me." I emit a halfhearted guffaw.

My words don't seem to register with Jack as he stands transfixed by the massive animal between us.

"Hey, Hercules," I say waving at him. "You're not cracking, are you?"

"Fuck you, bro," he says, turning toward me. "This is fucked on so many levels. Totally fucked. What do you think we can do here, now, ever?"

Jack and I had initially bonded over our shared brand of gleeful cynicism that was a distinct contrast to the starry-eyed idealism that seemed to permeate the attitudes of our peers in the Peace Corps. Something in his tone told me that this wasn't just another jaded tongue-in-cheek comment.

"Let's get this over with," I say, grabbing the legs.

It is dusk by the time we drag the cow to the treeline along the far side of the pasture. There, we are joined by a group of barefoot, adolescent village children who are carrying smoldering cow patties, which emit plumes of thick white smoke. They quickly arrange more smoldering dung in a circle around the suffering beast. Jack and I take off our veils. I pretend not to notice when he wipes his glassy eyes.

The children methodically scrape the stingers from the cow's hide with kitchen knives they've brought from their houses. Without the stingers, I see that the cow is dappled brown and white. Its breathing is jagged and irregular.

"Hey, I have an idea," I say, pulling an EpiPen from my pocket. "What do you think? Do you have yours?"

Jack rifles through his pocket and hands me his auto-injecting adrenaline shot. All the beekeeping volunteers were given one on the first day of our Peace Corps training.

"Where do I put it?" I ask, popping the safety cap.

"How should I know?" Jack says. "Somewhere soft."

"Didn't you grow up on a farm?" I say.

"My dad sold farm insurance," he says. "We leased our land to almond farmers. I don't know anything about cows."

"How about here?" I ask, stroking the coarse hair on its neck. "It's soft here."

Jack nods and I stab the cow with the EpiPen. Almost immediately she takes a deep breath and her breathing becomes more normal.

"Holy shit!" I say, smiling. "It worked!" The children whistle and cheer in Guaraní—a language that is still very foreign to me.

Before long, we are joined by some local farmers who cluster around Jack. They have nicknamed the giant American "Ivan." The way they say it, the name sounds like "Ee-bahn."

"Ivan, you saved the cow," one farmer says in Spanish.

"Ivan, you carried it yourself," suggests another, patting him on the bicep. "You can carry a cow!"

Ivan is short for Ivan Drago, famed Russian antagonist of the Rocky movies. It turns out that everyone in Paraguay has seen Spanish-dubbed versions of *Rocky IV*. It does not matter that, except for blonde hair, Jack looks nothing like Dolph Lungdren. All the American beekeeping trainees in the village think the nickname is hilarious, except for Jack, of course.

In broken Spanish, Jack insists that the cow is still in a precarious condition. The nuance of his comment is either lost or ignored because the villagers have decided that they have just witnessed the sort of valor that they have come to expect from the Americans that they see in their favorite Spanish-dubbed Hollywood action movies.

While Jack chats with the villagers, I squat over the cow's massive head. The stingers have been mostly scraped from her body, but her breathing is already beginning to become labored again.

"Peter!" Jack exclaims, grabbing me by the shoulder, his voice bright for the first time that evening. "Did you hear that, Peter?"

"What?"

"They have called for the veterinarian!" he cries. "Peter, we might actually save her!" It is too dark to see his face, but I can tell from his voice that he is excited about this news.

"Look, you stay here," he says, his voice brimming with determination. "I'll go to all of the beekeepers in our group and get their EpiPens and bring them back. We just need to keep her alive until the veterinarian gets here. Give her my shot if her breathing becomes labored again, okay?"

I sit vigil over the suffering cow until the vet arrives on the back of a motorbike. He is a middle-aged balding man who is indistinguishable from the villagers in his tattered shorts and flip flops. He seems neither surprised nor particularly interested when I explain, in broken Spanish, that I had administered six human doses of adrenaline to the cow to keep it alive. He nods sagaciously and deftly pours a big bottle of antihistamine down the cow's throat.

"What do you think, doctor?" I say in Spanish, when he has finished force feeding the medicine. "Is she going to live?"

The vet says something in Spanish that sounds both complicated and technical, but I decide the tone is hopeful.

"Let's go grab a drink, Jack," I say, slapping my gigantic friend on the back. "I'm buying."

We go to the one home in the village where we have seen folks gather to drink ice-cold Pilsen beer. The proprietor, Carlito, is a paunchy, curly-haired young man with a gregarious wife and a throng of smiling children. He has arranged a variety of patio furniture in front of his house where customers can sit and drink frosty 40-ounce beers poured into glass jars under a flood light that illuminates his front yard.

"I make this toast to the great Ivan Drago," I say, holding a jar of beer in the air, "the myth, the man, the legend of Cumbarity—who single handedly snatched an enormous beast from the jaws of death."

"And I toast Pedro Jones," Jack says ebulliently, "the man whose quick-thinking actually saved the day!"

Jack drinks beer like water and I do my best to keep up. We drink long into the evening, and, with every bottle, our toasts become increasingly outlandish and ridiculous:

"To the Samson of Cumbarity!"

"To Hippocrates Jones!"

"To the Brawn of Berkeley!"

"To Doctor Livingstone, I presume!"

It takes six or eight of the 40-ounce Pilsen bottles before Jack begins showing any effect from the beer. His words slurring, Jack leans in close to me to share a confession. "I was beginning to think everyone was right," he says wistfully, his big freckled brow furrowed.

"Right about what?" I ask hiccupping.

"That I was not coming for anything," he explains. "But that I was just running away from my responsibilities. Coach, my dad, everyone said it. They had a whole intervention."

I nod because I can feel the mood shifting, though the truth is that I'm not sure I completely understand what he is saying. It feels like our friendship is too new to ask too many clarifying questions.

"What did your parents say," Jack asks, "when you told them that you were coming to Paraguay?"

"Everyone thought I had gone mad," I lie. The truth is that only my friends from college thought it was crazy that I joined the Peace Corps. My parents, on the other hand, were old hippies whose lifelong counsel to me had been to be "true to myself." Their support for my decision to spend two years teaching beekeeping in Paraguay had always been enthusiastic and unqualified.

"My whole life, all I wanted to do is get a job working with animals, whether it meant becoming a veterinarian, a biologist, or just a farmer," Jack says, almost as if to himself. "And everyone pretended like they supported my goals. I majored in fucking biology for God's sake. Do you know how fucking hard organic chemistry is? And I passed it while playing football for a good D1 program! Did they think I was taking those classes for fun?"

I nod, wide-eyed, as if I know how hard it is to pass biology classes at Cal.

"But as soon as I make a decision to actually do what I said I wanted to do, everyone acts like I've lost my mind. They say I have a 'responsibility' to go into the NFL draft," he says making air quotes with his massive hands. "What about a responsibility to myself? What about a responsibility to my dreams?"

"Fuck 'em," I say, waving my hand as if to dismiss these naysayers.

"Yeah, fuck 'em!" Jack cries, raising his jar of beer. "Saving that cow today made me realize that I am right where I'm supposed to be."

"A toast for the cow!"

"Hear, hear!"

I am very hungover the next day and have a hard time concentrating in my intensive language classes, which are scheduled for four hours every morning. I endure a seemingly endless series of exasperated sighs from my Guaraní language teacher, who can't seem to understand why I am having so much trouble remembering the greetings that I had recited effortlessly the day before. I am saved from this torture in the mid-morning, by Don Antonio, the Director of the Agriculture Sector Programs, who is also the only Paraguayan national in a leadership position in the main offices in Asuncion.

Don Antonio is a jocular, stout middle-aged man with a meticulously groomed coif of thick salt-and-pepper hair and an unabashed reputation as a consummate ladies' man. He does not seem to be in a joking mood and leads me to his gleaming white Land Rover with the Peace Corps logo emblazoned on the door. Jack is already standing there—having been summoned from his language class too.

"Okay, gentlemen," he begins in his Spanish-accented English, glowering, "who gave the EpiPens to the cow?"

I raise my hand.

"*Idiota*," he spits. "They aren't for animals."

"But Don Antonio—"

He puts his hand up to shush me.

"Each of those EpiPens costs more than it would cost us to buy a new cow for the family," Don Antonio explains.

"But we saved—" Jack interjects.

"The cow is dead!" Don Antonio cries. "You did nothing except to cost our program thousands of dollars. We were very clear in our training that you are to use—oh, Jesus Christ, man. Pull yourself together."

But it is too late. Jack is blubbering like an enormous child. I pat him on the back and flash a withering glare at Don Antonio. Before long, some villagers and a few other beekeeping trainees have gathered to watch aghast as Jack cries hard, convulsing and sputtering, into his enormous hands. The scene is mildly terrifying: a giant man losing all composure like that. I am stuck in the awkward position of patting him on the back, while at the same time trying not to look at him during the public humiliation.

When he exhausts himself weeping, everyone sheepishly pretends like nothing notable has transpired.

By that afternoon I get word that Jack has quit the Peace Corps. He leaves without saying goodbye to anyone, including me.

A few days later, I walk past a group of kids playing on the street on the outskirts of the village. They are gleefully throwing clumps of dirt from the road into a nearby ditch, where the fetid, bloated carcass of the cow is being consumed by vultures and thick, pulsating swarms of black flies. The scene is both mesmerizing and awful.

For the first time since his unceremonious departure, I feel a twinge of relief that Jack has gone back home.

Young Adult Novel Excerpt

Judge — Joyce Sweeney
Coral Springs, Florida
"I was so impressed with the high level of work from your entrants!"

First Place
Dark White
Ruth Andrews — Cassopolis, Michigan

1 Wannabe

We sit in the window booth, our eyes on the vacant storefront across the street, using mind control to make the artist appear. We are Diva Davis and Katya Klassen, sixteen years old, cocked and ready for action.

"Think he's a Big Artist?" I ask Diva, the self-appointed authority on almost everything.

"Medium. If he was big we'd have heard of him." Her slanty brown eyes suddenly widen. "You're not actually—"

"Oh, yes. *We* are. Going to meet him."

"Then I guess ..." She points at my head.

"Gah!" I rip off my hairnet and shake my dark-brown hair into its bob, glancing around to see if anyone noticed. Luckily, it's midafternoon and Rocco's is empty. We just biked back from working the lunch shift at Whispering Pines. "Why can't I remember?"

"Cause you live in Kay-Kay Land." Yesterday a man kissed me. My coach.

He got in the water and put his hands on me to correct my stroke. Watery reflections danced on his chest. He kissed me on

the mouth and said he'd make me into a champion.

My lips buzzed. Electricity shot through me, my knees buckled, my feet came off the bottom and I sank underwater laughing. When I came back up his handsome face was scary-mean. "You can be my girl, so long as no one knows. No one." Coach is twenty-two, a senior at State. Every single girl on swim team is in love with him.

"You girls want the radio on?" yells Jackie, the owner of Rocco's and the biggest mouth in Three Oaks.

The oldies come on and we sing in British to *Sergeant Pepper's Lonely Hearts Club Band.* Accents are our thing. Diva points to the greasy salt-and-pepper shakers between us. "Salt and pepper. That's where Paul got the idea."

"How could you possibly know that?"

"Salt and pepper, just like you." Jackie sets root beer floats in front of salty white me and peppery dark Diva. Jackie'd probably tell an amputee they were missing a leg. She's older than our moms but unlike them she didn't let herself go. "You know, you're a good singer," she tells Diva, as if Diva wasn't the star soloist of People's Protestant Youth Choir. And to me, "You heard about the new guy? They say he's gonna turn Three Oaks into an Artist's Colony."

"Seriously?" If *I* lived in an artist colony… Coach wasn't talking about the dolphin kick when he said it's all about the rhythm. Maybe he and I… my head swirls with pre-carnality.

Jackie brings herself down to our eye level. "When all them artists start movin' in? I'll have to get me an espresso machine!"

She bursts out laughing and sashays off to *You're such a lovely audience.*

Diva says boom bada boom, her eyes on the butt-dimples in Jackie's pink stretch pants. "Jackie couldn't tell a Van Gogh from a Gauguin," I hiss-per. "Anyway," I challenge Deedy, "I'll bet the only Big Artists you know are dead."

"Salvador Dali."

"Dead."

"Yoko Ono."

"Cheater. You never would've thought of her if the Beatles weren't playing."

"Darling, being aware of the ambience is hardly the same as cheating."

"Darling, shove it up your ass-i-ance."

A battered pickup rolls to a stop in front of the artist's building and practically spits the driver into the street. I half-rise, straining to see. Scrawny and hunched, he unlocks the door to the building and goes inside.

Diva moans, "He's *skinny*. Who made it a rule that artists have to be skinny?" She looks at me accusingly, and then down at herself. "I look like a pear with arms and legs."

"You've got curves plus you're gorgeous. I look like a snake with a toad in its mouth."

"A snake with BBs."

She calls my boobs BBs because they're big. "That was unnecessary." The artist comes out, lowers the tailgate, and pulls a dolly off the truck.

Diva says, "Forty. At least."

"C'mon." I scoot out of the booth, scared but determined. The chances of me blowing this are better than never being struck by lightning. Plus, I'm not good at rejection. But today is

July 21st, 2008. I've lived in Three Oaks, Ohio, population twelve hundred, almost my entire life and it's killing me. I throw a fist into the air, "Seize the day."

Diva doesn't budge. She sits there searching for a way to explain something terribly basic. "You can't barge into someone's life like a bull in a china shop."

A red cape waves before my eyes, horns rise from my skull and my nostrils flare. Diva gives a little scream and shrinks back. I sigh and revert, "Deedy, you know I'm a Taurus. And, anyway it's not fair. Think about it. If you're on *Jeopardy!*, you win the prize. If you're a singer, which you are, it's more subjective but you can still win *American Idol*. But what if you're an artist?" I raise my palms to the ceiling. "Nobody ever believes you. Nobody knows what's good."

A sweet little frown creases her brow. "*I* believe you. You *are* good." Her big gold hoops sway with belief. It means a lot.

I blow her a kiss. "Because you love me, but you're not artistically qualified to have an opinion." She's silent. I give her credit because she doesn't normally let anyone disqualify her from anything. "See? I need a real artist."

Her eyeballs drift up and off, but she's smiling. "Whatever. Let's do this thang."

***

We cross Main, floats in hand. The artist is searching for something in the bed of his truck. Diva whispers, "The dude has no butt."

I giggle. Flirtatiously. And fail to make it onto his radar screen. He jumps out of the truck, jams a wedge under the door of his building, climbs back in, and puts a heavy box on the tailgate.

Diva makes a loud sucking noise with her straw. He looks up and through us. Shorter than me with close-set eyes and a head that juts from his shoulders. Think rodent.

I make a ridiculously loud sucking noise. Diva harmonizes. He sees us. We smile. "You girls want to give me a hand?" His voice has a ratty twang.

I say okay and set my float on the sidewalk. Diva says she has to go and trots off. "Terrence Embry." He holds out his hand.

"Katya Klassen." His hand is so warm it's almost hot. Terrence Embry—the name sings—hoists himself into the truck and gives me boxes to stack on the dolly. He doesn't say much. When the boxes are three high and I'm cradling a fourth in my arms he jumps off, tips the dolly, and walks backward into the empty storefront. I follow. As he unloads, I veer with my box into the center of the long, empty room, look up at the patterned-tin ceiling, and revolve slowly, imagining the space full of painting and sculpture. This is my chance. I turn to him. "I want to be an artist."

I wait.

For him. To smile. Something. His rat-eyes glisten. "Why?"

Root beer sloshes in the pit of my stomach. Anything I say will be wrong. "I like to draw."

"Of course you want to be an artist," his fingers make air quotes. "Everybody does once. But they get over it, thank God, like the measles and the chickenpox." The quote ends and he heads back to his truck.

I drop my box with a thud. I am not some stupid wannabe. My great-grandpa was an artist, I've got art in my blood, I've got art in my body crying desperately to—he's pulling a ladder off the truck. I rush to catch the end before it hits the ground. "Who said that?"

"Gulley Jimpson. It's from *The Horse's Mouth*. Read it."

Damn him, I *will* read it. "And I can memorize paintings."

He stops—jolting me to a standstill, but in the split second before I put on the brakes, my momentum forces him to stagger-step. I can't see his face because he's inside the building, and I'm outside in the sun. He says, "What?"

"I've already learnt five. Right now I'm memorizing a Kerry James Marshall."

"How the fuck do *you* know Kerry James Marshall?"

Dude, language. "Um, isn't he famous?"

"Hardly. I'll grant he's a genius, but he's maybe had one show. In Chicago."

My eyes have adjusted to the glare and I can see he's truly confounded. "Well, the librarian gave me his catalog. For free." Gadzilla, I actually recognized genius. I search Terrence Embry's face for evidence I've come up a notch.

"And just how do you mem-o-rize a painting?"

I ignore his mocking tone. "You stare at it without thinking. After a while something starts to stand out. That thing is the key; it explains the colors and shapes and everything. I start with a pencil sketch, then do it again with pastels or watercolors." I give him my seductive smile, *now* he knows who he's dealing with.

He starts us walking again. "These paintings you memorize, they're from the internet?" His voice has lost its smirk.

"Art books from the library. Mom says we're getting internet next month." We lean the ladder against a wall, return to the truck, unload a heavy saw on a stand followed by canisters that look like the missiles in spy cartoons. I ask no questions because

I don't want to seem ignorant. There's a miter box, a box labeled Boomerangs, two stools, more boxes, a roll of butcher paper, and a bicycle. "You bike?"

"I'm addicted." He actually sounds happy. "Are there any bike paths around here?"

"No, but I can show you how to bike around the lake. It's kind of tricky 'cause of the cul-de-sacs."

He throws back his head and barks. I guess that's how he laughs. "That would be great, Katya, but I won't be back till Saturday. I'm giving a workshop on Pelee Island." He rummages in his pocket and fishes out a ten, "Thanks for helping me today."

Is he trying to get rid of me? "I wasn't helping you for money." I sound desperate. He presses the ten into my hand. "Make me happy, okay?"

The warmth of his hand proves that when you have art inside you, you heat up. Terrence Embry has not seen the last of Katya Klassen.

Second Place
Coronation
Laura Thompson — Nashville, TN

I. *Paris, November 1398*

"You have my answer."

They stood warming their hands over a brazier, the smell of wet wool mingling with the charcoal smoke and the fainter, stale scent of the heavy drapes and tapestries. The shutters were closed against the cold. Lord Salisbury unpinned his cloak and his page removed it. "I was certain we would come to some agreement, Sir Joseph. Of all his men, I sought you first. You must take time to reconsider—I will not press you now."

Joseph stepped away from the brazier and dismissed the boy, who was waiting to take his cloak as well. He said to Salisbury, "There is nothing to consider."

Lord Salisbury had approached him with utter confidence and seemed never to have imagined the possibility of refusal. He was one of the wealthiest men in England, and if Joseph was known at all to the court, he was known to be poor, barely able to maintain himself in arms and horse. Now Salisbury's brow creased, and his voice was almost pleading. "I fear I have offended you. Let me be clear: the knowledge I seek from you would by no means impinge upon your honor, or your duty to Lord Henry. What I have offered is a unique chance to serve your king."

"My lord. What you have offered is a great deal of money to spy on my friends."

"If your friends are loyal, as they continue to protest, then your confirming their intentions can only help them. The king means to do justly by his cousin, but for that he must be completely informed. Your reputation as an honest man, Sir Joseph, a sober and discreet young man, was what most recommended you to me. Only think how by your good assistance, you may well win your lord reprieve from exile."

"Now you stray into conjecture, Lord Salisbury. You will not persuade me, and I must take my leave of you."

"You are the kind of man the king could love," Salisbury said as Joseph waited for the boy to unbolt the door. "Don't bury your own life together with the ruin of Lancaster. Henry may be a noble lord and a good master, but you will never prosper if you stay with him."

"Truly, my lord, your concern for my personal affairs is magnanimous, and I am sorry to disappoint you. No doubt you will find others just as worthy to accept that purse."

Joseph went out into a fine rain, letting the wind off the Seine scour him. If cold and water could have washed the creeping feeling of contamination from his skin, he would have dived into the river. The fresh air in his lungs did something to displace his anger, but the rottenness of Salisbury's proposal lingered.

He went directly to Lord Henry at the Hôtel de Clisson. At last divested of his sodden cloak, he stood with his back to the blazing fireplace, both hands wrapped around a pewter cup of hot spiced wine. He made his report briefly, concluding, "We may be sure the king will have his agent in your household soon enough."

"He's had us watched since we left London," Lord Henry said. He was a tall man, handsome and well-made, but grief and agitation had deepened the lines around his eyes. He was thirty-two but looked older. His voice, however, was warm and resonant, his tone almost lighthearted. "Unless he's paid his spies to murder me, I have nothing to fear from them. Are you hungry? There's seed cake, if you want it. Oranges as well, fresh from Spain."

"The consolations of exile." Joseph acknowledged the food, set out in silver dishes on a sideboard, but remained by the fire.

Henry went on, "I have done nothing against King Richard, and continue to do nothing. To do nothing, and be witnessed doing nothing, is the utmost reach of my ambition these days. I rather wish you had accepted Salisbury's purse."

"I am not yet so destitute as to need his thirty pieces of silver."

"I only meant," said Henry, grasping his shoulder, "that it might have been useful to have a man in the king's pay, quite beyond the financial implications for you, considerable as they may be. But of course I could not ask you to undergo such risk on my behalf, unless you were entirely willing."

"Whatever man he buys will be no friend to you. I knew that risk, as well, when I refused him." Joseph drank some wine and turned toward the fire, shoulder-high as it consumed a massive log. "I do not think, though, that the king intends to murder you, only to keep you in his sight. Quite possibly he wants you well aware that you are being observed."

"He has taken Harry into his household," Lord Henry said, and the queasy sense of having tasted poison ran through Joseph again.

"Your son's life for your good behavior?"

"That would be far too easy. More likely he'll dazzle the boy with generosity and kindness, and by degrees turn him against me. But one never knows with Richard."

"I could not play the part successfully," said Joseph. "No one who knows me would believe in a conversion so extreme."

"Did Lord Salisbury believe he could convert you?"

"I suppose he must have. He seemed to think I would be grateful for a chance to distinguish myself in the king's service."

"None of the king's men know you. You are the youngest of my knights here, and your name is not yet firmly linked with mine. If any of the others went over to King Richard now, it would seem strange, but you—you might plausibly regret having followed me into exile, and be grateful for the chance to redeem both your fortunes and your loyalty. That, surely, is what Salisbury anticipated."

"If I did accept him," said Joseph, tossing the dregs of his cup onto the fire, "what would you have me do? Report your hunting parties with the dukes of France, your attendance at debates on the Church schism?"

"Assure them of my loyalty. Entice them with a few choice truths that otherwise I might have kept hidden. Eventually, perhaps, convince them to revoke my banishment."

"And, of course, report to you whatever I may glean of events in England."

"There you have it."

"Salisbury will wonder why I've changed my mind."

"Well, the purse, man. That would weigh heavily on anyone's conscience."

II. *London, March 1399*

i.

It was like old times. They were the same men, their faces bright with fellowship and drinking, their voices joined in shouts and singing. On the table were the pitchers of grassy beer, the plates of salted radishes, the lamps that made the air around them waver with the flame's heat. It was all the same, except that the men's badges now were harts and crosses where once they had been flowers and swans: the emblems of their changed allegiance.

Joseph had not been expected, and his friends' response when he arrived at their table threatened to usurp any dignity yet left to the occasion. Returning a few greetings and handshakes, but refusing to answer any questions, he took his old place on the bench beside Gilles. "You met tonight to say farewell, and not welcome. Don't let me interrupt. Do the late duke justice, and I'll drink to him with you."

"If his death has brought you home," said Gilles, glowing golden in the lamplight as he slid a tankard into Joseph's hand, "well, there's our consolation. To the noble duke, in whose service our eternal bonds of friendship first were forged. He was a second father to many of us, and we will not forget him."

Up and down the table, voices intoned, "The duke of Lancaster." The cups emptied and refilled, another man stood and made his salute. By the time half of them had spoken, both tears and laughter had intruded upon decorum, and at the far end of the table several of the brotherhood had given up drinking to the duke of Lancaster and were harmonizing on the theme of love's poisoned darts.

"They've sunk to new depths in your absence," Gilles said, throwing a heavy arm around Joseph's neck and knocking their cups together. "You never should have left us."

"Am I to blame for this?" The white hart on Gilles's badge was set with small gemstones, and one had caught on a loose thread in Joseph's sleeve. He held the badge in his hand for a moment after ripping it free. "Your little deer has bitten me." Then he laughed and pushed the pin back through the fabric of

Gilles's coat, where it hung limply askew. He raised his cup and said to the few who were still listening, "Our lord the duke of Lancaster. He was a true prince."

"The duke of Lancaster," said Gilles, draining his cup again. "And our good Lord Henry? Not quite so true and noble as his father, is he? Has it really been worthwhile, leaving us and all of this behind to serve him in exile?"

As Gilles reached for the pitcher to refill his tankard, someone knocked against his arm, and the beer flowed across the table. The men beside them scrambled out of the way, shouting for towels and a new pitcher. His voice dampened by the confusion, Joseph said, "If you want to talk about nobility, what of the king? In France, they said King Richard praised God for his uncle's death as for a blessing."

"It's a lie. What do the French know of it? The king was with Duke John at the end, and he felt the loss as much as anyone. No other lord can come close to old John of Gaunt for power and constant loyalty."

"Is that why you've put on the royal livery?"

"You must have known you'd find us wearing it. It's forty days since the duke died."

"I did not know I'd find so many of you. Were you bought at wholesale?"

"The king made us a generous offer, and after all, what choice did we have? It's not too late for you to join the household yourself, you know. Lord Henry has his other knights, and he couldn't need you as much as we do—for the Irish war."

Joseph tapped the white hart with his cup. "Can you see me wearing one of these?"

"Yours wouldn't be like this, exactly. I had the jewels added at a goldsmith's. You think it's obscenely gaudy, don't you?"

"The obscenely gaudy suits you, Gilles, though I will not say the same for the king's emblem. Look at its little collar, worked in carbuncles."

Their friends had roused the men at the next table to join in a drinking song, the pitcher passing from hand to hand until the verse's end, when whoever was holding it was required to drain it. It moved swiftly from Gilles to Joseph and then on down the bench. The singing turned to japes and goading, and the losing man drank until the beer was pouring down his beard onto his doublet and his own badge of the white hart.

Returning to their quarters some time later, the street quiet except for the incoherent voices of their friends walking some distance ahead of them, Gilles said, "The war in Ireland could be the making of your fortune. Not even Lord Henry would begrudge you that. Stay with us, Joseph. Come to Ireland."

Lamps glowed behind closed shutters, and lanterns flamed at every doorway, but it was not like speaking face to face in daylight. Their starkly outlined features, ever changing in the swells of ascending and descending shadow, made them look like strangers to each other. They crossed an alley, a gulch of darkness and unwholesome air, and Joseph answered, "I mean to come with you. Did I say otherwise?"

"By God, if you serve in the king's retinue, you'll prosper, I know it. The only thing is—"

"What?"

"The oath."

"To serve the king alone, for life? You know I cannot swear," said Joseph, and he caught a glimpse of Gilles's exasperation as they passed beneath an open shutter.

"Listen," Gilles said. "The king's steward, Worcester, is a relation—a distant one. A cousin of ours married a godchild of his, that sort of thing, but nonetheless, there's a connection. If you cannot see your way to making an exception to your principles, I'll vouch for you with him. He wouldn't deny a friend of mine."

"No," Joseph interrupted, then more quietly repeated, "No. I thank you, but I'll do it on my own."

"Don't be stupid," said Gilles. "You've never attempted to hide your loathing of the king, and if anyone began asking questions—or if you answered in your usual attitude—"

"What do you take me for? I will come humbly, renouncing all my former sayings and affiliations, begging the king's pardon for them if need be. I have no need of anyone's support or recommendation. We were all Lancaster's knights, once, and if they have taken the rest of you into the king's affinity, they will take me as well."

"You're the only one who chose to go with Lord Henry when the king banished him."

"And thus the only one to have demonstrated true obedience to the king's authority."

"Yes, say that. I hope they will believe you. Here's the sign of the Lion," said Gilles. He pounded on the shuttered door, and they stood waiting for someone to answer.

"You're sure you won't come with me to Margery's? She'll have a bed made up for you in the shop, and you'll be far more comfortable."

"If Margery learns I'm back, then Bess will hear of it, and break her heart again. I hope I can trust you to say nothing to her, Gilles. Let both of them continue to believe I am in France."

"Please yourself, but you're a fool. Lent or no, if I were you, I'd be in Bess's bed tonight," said Gilles, as the door heaved open and a lantern dazzled their eyes.

"No doubt you would. Is that you, Bénigne?"

"Sir Joseph," said a voice behind the lantern-light.

"Bénigne!" Gilles cried in delight. "Are you still following this mumbler from one end of the world to the other, into exile and back again?"

"Sir Gilles, God grant you everlasting life," said Bénigne dryly.

Gilles laughed and said, "A good night will suffice at present. I'll come for you in the morning, Joseph, shall I? By God, I'm glad you're back. We'll bury the good duke together."

ii.

They heard the Requiem Mass at Carmelites in Fleet Street, then followed the procession to Saint Paul's. A sharp breeze lashed the mourners and whistled past rooftops and trees, bright sun and gusting rain ceding the air to one another in swift and ceaseless barter.

Inside the cathedral, the wind's howl rose faint but audible above the chanted harmonies of the divine service. The vastness of the transept's height belittled what was human in the scene below. Shoes and robes dripping onto chill stone, the ranks of mourners shrank beneath the shadows of the soaring walls and bowed their heads before the tomb of John of Gaunt, duke of Lancaster.

The coffin, draped in rich fabric depicting the royal arms, had been laid before the altar amidst a galaxy of burning candles. In alcoves and on monuments all around it, statues slept, slender stone hands folded in supplication on armored breasts. The duke's hands had been broad and powerful, heavy on a small boy's shoulders. Joseph had lost his own father too young to have much memory of him, but he remembered how the duke had pulled him close and told him he must pray for the salvation of his father's soul. The duke had thanked him, a child of four or five, for his father's brave and loyal service, and had sworn that he would never be without a home or family while John of Gaunt lived.

In the presence of death, substance seemed to waver and dissolve. Even the boy choristers and the stairstep row of ducal grandsons, narrow shoulders overwhelmed by their black robes, carried a premonition of dust and bones in their thin white faces.

But at the summit of the choir, King Richard sat serene, a graven image, cold eyes open through the ages. Death could not touch him, and he held power over all their lives. He had not killed the duke of Lancaster, but in surviving him he had triumphed. Lancaster's claim upon the crown became irrelevant. The duke lay beyond influence or intercession. King Richard could reduce his heirs and his dependents to ruin or to reinvention, as he wished. Only the king's will mattered now, and his unnatural detachment as he observed his victory was horrible.

Dread hollowed Joseph's body like hunger. The polyphony wandered into dissonance, the pure beauty of children's voices only magnifying the horror woven into the opposing lines. Was it prophetic insight that made him see death everywhere he looked, or only sorrow and discomfort? The worldly urgencies of aching cold and heavy damp, rasping lungs and shrieking wind, obscured the hope of resurrection and salvation. If life were nothing but a shadow, its darkness loomed out of proportion, overwhelming all except for momentary glimpses of a higher truth.

Third Place
Wild and Precious Life
Kathleen Laufenberg — Tallahassee, FL

Chapter 1: Shhh

As Dad snores, I tiptoe out the front door and scurry for the Sky Bridge.

Both elegant and practical, our glass-and-steel Sky Bridge connects Prime Numbers, the high-rise where my father and I and the other senior scientists and their families live, to the Lab complex, where everyone works. Strolling across it, I feel eerily suspended in the air. Outside, beneath a nearly full moon, the aspens and pines glisten from a midnight rain. Their water-freckled leaves and dripping needles merge with the shadows to create a darkly magical effect—and I could use a little magic in my life right now.

From the tree-line, a doe steps into the moonlight. Her tan-and-white tail twitches as she ambles toward the sprawling GenTech compound. Pressing against the cold glass, I marvel at her wild beauty: her alert ears, her graceful neck, her sleek body.

"Run," I whisper, my breath fogging the glass. "Run, B-Beauty! Before they come for you, too."

Almost as if she'd heard, the deer looks toward the woods.

My watch vibrates, telling me it's already 2:30; I should get going. When I glance back up, the doe is gone.

*****

With an ominous *thunk*, the door to my father's lab shuts behind me.

I jog past the darkened silhouettes of refrigerators and freezers, and then the less recognizable stuff: the squeeze cages, swivels for tethering, biopsy punches and organ baths. My father's lab thrums with a quiet machine power, a white-noise so pervasive most people forget it's there. But I don't. For me, it's a constant reminder of the Lab's sinister side.

When I reach Dad's office, I key myself in. In order to learn the dates of the next Harvest, I need to access his computer. Slipping into his squeaky leather chair, I type P-A-D-D-I-E.

Unbelievably, he's still using my name as his password. Why one of his top nerds hasn't told him to change it, I haven't a clue. Or maybe I do. They're probably too intimidated.

Dad's personal calendar unfolds until *bingo!* there it is: a big 'H.' My heart hammering, I pinch and spread open the screen until an info box unspools, a lotus opening its petals.

The next Harvest begins October 21. Today is the 19th. So, in *two* days? My best friends are scheduled for Harvest in 48 hours?

Scowling at the screen, I squeeze the arm rests in a death grip. To my father and his team, Mango and Seven are just vessels. OTVs, they call them: Organic Transplant Vessels. A means to an end. But to me, they're so much more.

As my heart races, my thoughts begin ricocheting into each other, like cars colliding on the interstate. Remember what the counselor said, I remind myself. Count your breath. Slow. It. Down. Concentrate on a sound, or an image, or a peaceful place.

The framed photo beside my father's computer offers me a focal point: a picture of my dad, my mom, and me, when I was little. We're at the beach—my first time ever—and we're all beaming like it's Christmas morning or something. It was taken before Mom got sick, and before Dad got whatever he is now.

Cold. Distant. Half-empty. But instead of lifting my spirits, it starts raining inside me: big fat drops pelting me from head-to-toe. I rub the heart-shaped locket around my neck. When my mother wore it, a tiny photo of me nestled inside it. Now it holds her picture.

What should I do, Mom? My eyes squeeze tight. Please help me.

My only answer is the buzz of the machines. Eventually I realize that if I intend to visit them, I gotta get moving. As I rummage inside my crossbody bag for reassurance that I haven't forgotten their treats, my goodie bag pops open. Its sweet aromas uncurl, and in my mind's eye, I see Seven's pink-lipped grin when she spots her green grapes, and Mango's golden eyes when he sniffs his beloved fruit. Inside me, the rain slows to a drizzle and stops.

Carefully, I restore everything on Dad's desk to pre-me. After locking up, I thread my way through an array of chairs, desks, and a chalkboard so riddled with formulas I can taste the limey dust. When I reach the last restricted area separating me from Mango and Seven, my fingers fumble at the security pad. The door responds with an angry *beep*.

Slow down, Paddie. The codes haven't changed. You entered the wrong digits.

I re-enter my father's access codes (correctly this time) and dip my black-market eraser in the digital lock. The flashing red light morphs to yellow then green, and I shoulder through the cold steel door. Inside the PPE (Personal Protective Equipment) room, I zoom past bin after bin of us-them crap: face shields and gloves, hair caps and plastic coats. Upon reaching the habitation chamber, I insert Dad's chip and enter yet another string of code.

Click. The final door releases. Thanking the dear, deaf gods, I go in.

Chapter 2: I Am Light

The habitat is in sleep mode, and my movements trigger minimal lighting. In here, the only sounds are Seven's intermittent snores and the rumble of the ventilation system. Despite its giant air scrubbers, a sharp urine tang never leaves this place. You get used to it, I suppose, the same way you get used to everything around here.

Well, sort of.

My first stop is the lone 22-foot cathedral cage that is Mango's enclosure. Dim light falls through its thick, jail-house bars, but I see no movement.

"Hey, b-b-buddy." Wait—I'm stuttering around my *friends* now? Colossal.

From my cross-bag, I remove Mango's treat and hold it aloft. With my free hand, I touch my lips, signing eat.

A dark figure rises from the top branch of what I call the Franken-tree, the plastic monstrosity bolted to the center of his cage. Mango leaps from it, landing with a *thrump* on the floor. Squatting like a simian Buddha, he eyeballs me.

Using my pocket knife, I slice open the golden fruit. Its tropical scent teases my nose—which means he smells it fifty-fold.

Sweet, I sign. "Mmmm," I add, egging his desire. "Dee-lish." Mango leaps to the front of the enclosure.

Eat now! he signs, his amber eyes lit with fire.

I plop half of the fruit in his metal food-box and push it in. He snorts and looks away—my cue to begin our night-time greeting. I unlock his cage, retrieve the mango and, like a humble servant, offer it on my outstretched palm. Circling my free hand over my heart, I sign *please.* He nods. Our ritual is complete.

"Do you want me to cut it up?" I pantomime the task.

Mango shakes his head no. We sit side-by-side beneath the Franken-tree, my green sweater pressing against his brown hair. I get a whiff of the fruit as he scoops it out with his fingers and plops it in his mouth. The smells of sweetness and sweat and sadness envelope me. I hug him as he eats his favorite treat, flooded with feelings of connection and impending loss. He pauses to touch my face with his sticky fingers, then returns happily to his beloved snack.

When he's done, I offer him the second half. He shakes his head no and points instead at my pocketknife. I'm surprised. He's seen me use this same knife a hundred times or more, and he's never asked to hold it.

"You want *this*?" Alarm tingles through me. "It's sh-sharp, Mango. Look." I touch the blade tip to my palm, make an exaggerated gasp. He leans in, brows furled, but when he sees that my hand is fine, he makes his soft "oot-oot" noise. Again he points his black fingernail at my knife.

My hazel eyes meet his golden ones. In the subdued light of the cage, I see only my friend. I close the knife. I circle a hand over my heart, *please*, then tap my index fingers together, signing *careful*. Breathless, I hand him the knife, refusing to think about how much trouble I'd be in if my father ever suspected I did such a thing.

Mango opens it, closes it, and opens it again. He smells it, then touches the tip of the knife's blade to his palm. His eyes widen.

"Told you," I say.

He takes the other fruit-half from me and cuts off a small piece. Making his throaty laughs, he hands it to me. He knows I love mango almost as much as he does.

"Okay, Mr. Smarty Pants," I say and take a big, juicy bite. "Mmm." Mango hoots and returns my knife.

I blow him a kiss, the sign for *thank you.*

When we've finished eating, the second part of our nighttime ritual begins. I put my arm around Mango's shoulders, and he curls into me just as he did when he was little. From my shoulder bag, I take out his "snow globe," which I made using an olive jar. If you shake it, a flurry of gold glitter (meant to be sunlight) sprinkles down on a tiny plastic monkey and girl sitting under a baobab tree.

Mango shakes and shakes and shakes it while I rake my fingers through his hair. As I groom him, I sing our favorite song: "I Am Light," by India.Arie.

"I am not the things my family did. I am not the voices in my head. I am not the pieces of the brokenness inside."

I take a deep breath: "I. Am. Light."

When I've finished grooming him, Mango sets down the globe. He runs his bony fingers through my hair and divides it into three strands. When he finishes braiding them, I hand him a band to tie off the end. Mango grooms me because I'm his family. That's why he expects me to groom him, too, and to spend time with him, bring him treats and watch over him.

But oh, my dear, deaf gods, how much longer can I do even these simple things? How can I protect him from the Harvest?

Ugly memories stir inside me. I have to get us—me, Mango and Seven—out of here. Which leads me to wonder again why no one has responded to my encrypted e-mail? MY SOS? Don't the so-called animal rights people care about us?

I pull Mango closer.

Sleepy, he signs, drawing his hand down the front of his face.

I slip the globe back in my bag, as he's forbidden to have anything breakable. Retrieving his Mr. Monkey doll from the cage floor, I place it beside his foot. His long toes curl like fingers around the stuffed animal.

I cross my arms over my chest, signing *love,* and he does, too. With his Mr. Monkey bumping behind him, Mango climbs the Franken-tree. On his privacy platform, he tucks the doll to his chest and disappears inside his sleep crate.

I let myself out, his cage door *clunking* behind me. Just down the aisle, I hear one of Seven's long, quiet snores and feel a surge of envy for how soundly my girl can sleep. Except she's not a girl, of course. She's a pig.

I hate to say that, though, because so few humans value pigs. They don't know them, I guess. They only eat them. But Seven is cuddly and clever and loves to play. Before unlocking her cage, I check my watch: 4:23. *Ho-ly!* I need to get going—but I can't leave without spending a little time with her. I crawl into her warm nest and snuggle up, breathing in her smells of straw and buttery earth and sweaty pig.

"Hey, Boo." I give her a squeeze.

Her tail thumps, and her ease of being settles into me, as I knew it would. Whenever I curl up with her, the problems inside me melt away. Strange but true. So I guess it's no wonder that the next thing I know, I'm waking up in darkness, a stalk of straw jabbing my nose.

My watch reads 5:13. 5:13! Dear deaf gods! The lights brighten as I roll over.

"Get your b-butt in gear, Paddie!" I growl, scrambling to my feet. Seven's big head pops up. "Paddie?"

I stare. "Seven?"

Her head drops back down as she yawns and stretches her legs out, zombie-straight. What the ...?

"Seven! Did you just say my name?"

She bumps my hand with her snout, her way of saying pet me, love me, spoil me.

Stroking her automatically, I glance over at Mango's cage. He's clinging to the top of it, studying us.

"Did you hear that?"

"Oot-oot," he says softly.

I *am* going crazy. And it's 5:18! Freaky-freak-me! I should've been home 10 minutes ago. I back out like a crab and, as her cage auto-locks, Seven ambles to the front. I reach through the bars and pet her short, soft hair, the color of yams.

"Did you say my name earlier?" I whisper.

She unfolds her elephantine ears, too big even for her genetically oversized head. Seven stamps her front hoof once: our sign for *yes*.

"S-Say it again," I demand.

She skewers me with her blue eyes, then stomps her hoof twice: our sign for *no*.

"This is insane." I need to go, but my body doesn't respond.

Seven wags her un-curly tail.

Finally, my legs work enough to wobble over to Mango's cage. When I wrap my fingers around its bars, Mango does the same, his gold eyes meeting mine.

"I'm going crazy," I tell him.

He presses his forehead against the steel bars, and I do, too. Being with Mango and Seven makes me feel more of who I am. Or want to be. Or something.

When I pull away, the imprint of the bars stays on my forehead.

I point to myself, then arc my fingers through the air, signing *I go*.

Mango nods and presses the tips of his index fingers together: the sign for *careful*. "What?" I'm confused. Aren't I always careful?

"I gotta go," I say, more to myself than him. On autopilot, I sprint out of the habitat, through the PPE room and into my father's lab.

I streak past machine station after machine station until, heart bombs exploding inside me, I digitally erase all trace of my visit. Panting, I step into the hallway and slide down the wall. One small minute, that's all I need. One small minute to gather up the pieces of myself.

Breathe, Paddie.

Just breathe.

Nonfiction/Creative Nonfiction

Judge — Dr. Cheryl Jennings
Tallahassee, Florida

All of the authors had very promising submissions. I enjoyed reading them. No doubt, their creative writing took patience, persistence, and plenty of imagination. I congratulate them!

First Place
Deeper than African Soil
Faith Eidse — Tallahassee, Florida

MELTED HANDS
That multitude of molded hands
Holding out flowers to the azure skies
…a hidden source
Wells from their untainted palms.
- Jean-Joseph Rabéarivelo

I stepped up to a red mud hut at the leprosarium near Kamayala, Congo, carrying a wash basin and bar of soap in gloved hands.

"*Koko?*" A verbal knock, a pause before I entered the dim room. A woman moved on a bamboo cot, her bony frame draped in crusty cloth wrappers.

"*Ayy?*" Her thin voice trembled.

"*Yami, Ufudielo.*" It's me, Faith.

I had not seen this patient before, or if I had, she had not looked this low. She may have arrived an advanced case while I was completing grade nine at the American school in the capital, which was newly named Kinshasa. I was home for summer vacation, helping Mom with her nursing rounds.

I set down the basin and soap and shuffled blindly along the dirt floor, feeling with my shoes for uneven patches in the dirt floor, sticks of firewood, small animals.

"*Moyo Mama.*" Hello, Mama. I pulled off my rubber gloves, not wanting her to notice this barrier between us. In a shaft of white-hot, mid-morning sun, she raised an arm to shield her eyes against searing light. The leprosy bacillus that grew in the cool extremities—fingers, toes, knees, elbows, ears, nose, eyes—would not dull her shooting cortical pain until she went blind.

She lay on a bare woven mat and reached a contracted, molded hand, pushing uncertainly at my knee. Hers was a numb hand, so long dead to sensation that its muscles and tendons were paralyzed. Her bones, damaged by bumps and bangs, were being reabsorbed by the body, so that her fingernails grew on her knuckles.

I wanted to touch her reaching hand, grip its stiff form. The medical term Mom used was *mains-en-griffe*, claw-hand. Mom was right behind me with more water and soap, and I knew she would say—heard her say—"Faith, put those gloves on."

My breath caught and my pulse skipped a beat. My skin was blemished with nothing worse than acne and I felt immortal, even marble.

"Start on her feet." Mom often took one of her four daughters to work, to help us feel involved and to keep us near her. I set the basin down at the foot of the woman's cot and soaped my wash rag. Mom cradled the woman's hand, finding her pulse. "Have you eaten?"

"No, how can I eat if I can't get up?"

The woman's toes were shredded, brown tattered skin revealing jagged pink beneath. I gently held one foot at the heel and rubbed each toe with the soaped rag. Yellow, sulfurous pus oozed from several of the chewed-up stumps. I had never seen toes in such a state. The woman did not flinch. This was no accidental run-in with sharp stones.

Mom shifted her gaze from the woman's face and stared at the toes. "Who did this to you?"

The woman folded both arms over her face and mumbled something.

"Pardon?" Mom asked. "Did a person do this to you?" From pregnancy to planting and harvesting, to pounding manioc into flour, women were this region's heavy labor. Was Mom asking whether someone had beaten her for her disability?

"*Kaaaa*," the woman wailed. "Rats do this."

Mom turned gray under her generous freckles.

The woman struggled to grasp a stout stick beside her. "I have this stick, but I don't know where they are until their teeth sink into good flesh."

Mom tried to lift the corners of the woman's wrapper to check the bites, but the cloth stuck. "Do you have another cloth?" she asked.

"There. It's dirty." The woman pointed with her chin to a corner of the hut.

Mom sent me outside with my bowl and soap to wash the wrapper and told the woman the rats would not bother her again. They would put down rat poison. I set the bowl on a stout chair and dipped a section of black crusted cloth into the water. I rubbed it with soap and scrubbed it to a lather between gloved knuckles.

From beneath the dirt, a gold and green pattern appeared. The worn cotton blurred under my eyes. A solid despair rose from the pit of my stomach. If infecting myself with leprosy would have eased the woman's suffering, I would have done it. Perhaps that's why I ignored the dousing I was getting through my gloves, the brown, mucous-laden water bathing an open cut on my hand.

This infection impulse was not unusual among survivors, especially in the days when Hansen's disease (leprosy) patients were separated from society, and families were divided. But immunity to the bacillus increases with age, and transmission is mainly to children by mucus, or through active lesions. Teenagers, due to cooler temperatures of extremities in puberty, are the most susceptible.

Mom emerged from the woman's hut, her jaw set, lips pursed.

"Can you buy rat poison?" I gave the wrapper one last rinse and wring out.

"Yes, we have some. We'll put it in the corners so people won't walk through it."

"Hey, look at this," I said, coming to my senses. "There's a hole in my glove."

Mom was typically cool and rational, so when she leaped to examine my hand, I jumped.

"Why didn't you tell me the gloves were leaking?" Then she saw the open sore. "Why didn't you tell me about the cut? I would never have let you help if I had known."

If there had been a spigot nearby, she would have doused my hand on the spot. But as it was, we would have to return to the clinic where rain barrels were hooked to indoor-outdoor taps.

Mom fell silent as we passed the spreading mango trees where a man and young boy sat in the shade. Several years back, a boy my age had run from the mission orphanage. He had raced the mile home to his mother at the leprosarium and my mom had not sent him back. She had started him on sulfone medicine. A white patch had appeared on the back of his shoulder. He couldn't see it but the other kids pointed and jeered. That Christmas grandma had come with quilts for the patients, handsewn by her friends in Canada, and the boy had received one for himself.

We walked up the steps into the tin-roofed, fieldstone clinic where the nurse, Izamo, was bent over a microscope, checking slides. He turned to greet us, brushing his hands on his white lab coat.

Mom nodded and rushed me to a stainless steel sink. "Wash your hands and soap them good—for a minute." She turned on a faucet and handed me a bar of soap.

Sparkling water poured out, splashing my cut. I sudsed my hands and washed between my fingers, under my nails and up over my wrists the way she'd taught me. Mom went to a shelf under the counter and rummaged for a large brown bottle of disinfectant. From this clinic, she and the nurse had given out the sulfone drug, DDS (diaminodiphenyl sulfone). Six months later, they had seen bacillus stop squirming and disappear from lesion scrapings. They had pronounced the Hansen's disease "arrested." Even though nerves would not regenerate, the bacillus had stopped growing.

Gradually, Mom and Izamo had handed out clean bills of health. But many patients stayed on, close to the clinic where they could get treatment for their wounds. Family came and went from the neat rows of sun-dried brick, thatch-roofed houses built in the mid-fifties by my father and the men of Kamayala. It was funded by the World Health Organization (WHO) to treat hundreds from southwestern Congo.

The disinfectant fizzed in my open cut, and Mom dabbed it with a sterile cotton ball. Then we told Izamo, "*Sala kabema,*" stay well, and walked our bikes through a sand puddle to the packed dirt road through tall savannah grasses.

"You know I'll have to put you on medicine," Mom said. "You mustn't breathe a word of this."

I nodded. I had no words anyway and no voice with which to say them. I would be a hidden leper, crouched in elephant grass, not breathing a word. The marble had cracked. I too could be watching my hands grow numb and retract like claws. How would I hold my pens and pencils? How would I write and draw? One of Mom's patients, the banana grower, no longer had fingers for tearing chunks of mush from a ball of *chindu.* Just stumps and an opposing half-thumb to grip it with.

Behind us a tire iron clanged on an old hub, Chief Dominque calling his people to a meeting. Over time he had gone from walking with a cane on numb, flapping feet, to crawling on his knees, his feet turned to toeless clubs, his walking muscles lost to the dead peroneal nerves of his inner thigh. Mom had made him rubber knee pads.

Women looked up from hoeing their beans, colorful pulses my mom had brought to improve their diets and give them a market crop. They waved at us and moved towards the ringing sound. A sweetly sorrowful melody rose from their thatch-roofed church, *Kuwakungu nyonga.* "Amid the trials that I meet, amid the thorns that pierce my feet, one thought remains supremely sweet, thou thinkest Lord of me."

We were many and we were one, hoeing our gardens, sitting on our beds each night, checking fingers and toes for nicks or burns, watching for lesions near elbows or knees, patches of pinkish-white, insensitive skin.

Deep into the night, while the moon rose over the savannah, Mom and Dad's low voices rose and fell behind their closed bedroom door. How could I have been so careless? It was as reckless as jumping off the cliff at the falls. If I had done something deliberately to get Mom's attention, it wouldn't have been more effective than this unthinking act. Yet I fell asleep knowing the woman was safe and wrapped in a clean cloth that night.

During the next six months, I guarded a pill bottle full of Dapsone, the tablet form of DDS. It was a large, white pill the size of a nickle. Its only measurable side-effect was the stuttering gulp required to swallow it, and the gag reflex that followed. Mom had warned me before I returned to school and settled into the Mennonite mission dorm, "There is still a lot of stigma about leprosy. You mustn't tell anyone, not even your sisters."

Hope would have been interested in my case, medically. Charity, whose scarred hands were still sensitive from her electrical burn, would have felt along with the "stigma" I felt. Either of them would have made great confidantes. But I believed Mom's warning and kept silent.

The solitary nature of my cure drove me to a secret obsession with leprosy. I counted myself a hidden patient, checking to see if my toes had curled into hammertoes as nerves fought off bacillus attacks and tendons shrank. I checked knees and elbows for numb, white patches, and felt my big nose to see if it had caved yet.

Perhaps it was in the library downstairs, I found *Who Walk Alone*, Perry Burgess's novel of a serviceman living in exile with leprosy. After his diagnosis in the US, he returned to the "sanctuary of sorrow," a leprosarium in the Philippines, and married his beloved Carita, also a patient. There was a lonely romance in the life of an exile, an added dimension to the everyday, an existence beyond the ordinary. Perhaps there was even a heightened awareness of other realities, a sense of living in another sphere, in tension with the world around you.

Later, I was gripped by a science fantasy character, Thomas Covenant the Unbeliever of *Lord Foul's Bane*. Thomas was created by a missionary kid like me whose father worked with lepers in India. Covenant was so cruelly shunned on the street for his leprosy that he slipped into a metaphysical state. He became one of the living dead, transported to a spiritual plane, though he was still living and breathing in the modern world. He called himself the Unbeliever because he dared not believe in this alternate world where he possessed a mystic power, white gold, against Lord Foul the Despiser.

It was the lepers' resilience in struggle that inspired Jean-Joseph Rabéarivelo, the great poet of Madagascar. He compared their hands to flowering cacti. "They say a secret spring rises in their leathery palms. An inner spring, they say, to slake the thirst of hordes of oxen and the thirst of many tribes, lost tribes, in the country to the South."

I discovered the "leper mass" conducted in the Middle Ages. It was a ceremony of symbolic burial, to comfort the lepers being ritually segregated from society. It reminded me of Dad's story that widows of our tribe were once expected to throw themselves into their husband's graves to show their grief. The medieval church required the patient, in rags, to follow in procession a cross-bearer and priests in ceremonial robes. From the cathedral to the cemetery, where a new trench had been dug, the leper went in a death march with her wailing family. There she stood at the lip of her own grave, taking part in her own funeral, hearing the final prayers for her soul, and the list of prohibitions that she must live under. She was to remain outside the city, ring a bell to warn on-comers, and hold out a pail on a stick to receive handouts.

I joined the procession of the living on the bus to school, chatted on the walkway, and shared cokes from the school store. I blanched a moment when the fizzy liquid burst on my tongue. How could I just hand the bottle on without a pang, or confession? Did I not care if my friends, Asifa or Jette, got leprosy? If I wiped the bottle on my skirt would they guess? And would that be enough? There was so much I feared if I told—friends turning their backs, walking away. There was so much I didn't know. Was my treatment just a precaution or was I actually infected and contagious?

I lingered after biology. Could I write an extra credit paper on Hansen's disease? Could I visit leprosariums and talk to doctors? My teacher grinned at first as though I were joking, but I persisted. He asked a dozen questions but finally said yes.

Mom had flown to the city and taken me to visit a hospital administrator at his home one evening. They discussed my case in soft tones under diffused lamplight. Mr. Robert Watalet, from Belgium, in white shirt and glasses, nodded. Yes, I must complete a full six-month course of Dapsone.

He ran the national leprosarium in Kinshasa, *L'Hôpital de la Rive,* stretched along an abandoned rail bed over-looking the lush Zaire River. Here, Mr. Watalet dispensed sulfone drugs, provided occupational therapy, and pioneered small industries to promote independence. His patients worked long hours, pushing numb fingers to perform exacting work like shoe-stitching and basket-weaving.

I was transfixed by the setting and the patients who seemed committed beyond their ability, sometimes using their teeth to grip and pull thin rattan fibers or raffia threads. Sweat beaded their hairlines, and ran around raised bumps on brow bones, noses, and lips. "Lepromatous nodules," I had read. Would I be willing to sit on the ground, sweating and forcing numb fingers to work?

Over Thanksgiving break, I hitched a ride home with my classmate, Amy, whose father, Dr. Wayne Meyers, was a microbiologist at a hospital known as Kivuvu, "place of hope," at Kimpese, "place of cockroaches." I followed Dr. Meyers through the cinder block building, while he chatted with patients and checked their noses and toes. He rebuilt sunken noses using a piece of the patient's rib. This was important for a person's dignity, he said, to walk in the market again and not be shunned. He introduced me to an orthopedic surgeon who restored tendons in feet and hands.

He examined the bumps that grew on the faces, ears, and hands of patients with lepromatus leprosy, and the flat, pinkish-white lesions of patients with tuberculoid leprosy. Some had a mix, flat lesions with bumpy borders, or borderline leprosy. Kimpese was a half-day drive from Kinshasa, but Dr. Meyers' patients got there any way they could.

Dr. Meyers took me to a large laboratory banked with microscopes, beakers, and petri dishes. He showed me slides of the three types of leprosy swimming in suspension and gave me time to draw pencil crayon images of the bacilli.

The Sunday night of our return to school, I swallowed my Dapsone tablet without gagging.

Decades later I was hired by the Department of Health, Office of Minority Health and Health Equity in Tallahassee, Florida. There, on early mornings, nine-banded armadillos scuttled into holes alongside roads and ditches. Clunky, prehistoric critters with an endemic leprosy rate of ten to twenty percent, they had become an immunology agent in the campaign against leprosy. At the end of 2018, there were 208,000 cases globally, down from 5.2 million in the 1980s. Worldwide, 16 million people have been cured of leprosy (WHO). Because of the rate of leprosy among native-born Texans, Louisianans and Alabamans, researchers continue to ponder the armadillo-to-human link. Was leprosy first transmitted to humans from armadillos, or the other way around?

For half a year I had crossed over into the Hansen's disease camp, swallowing tablets in secret and seeking out doctors and patients wherever I could. I was infected with a consciousness of displacement, amplified by adolescence, womanhood, and my traveling childhood. It became an inner spring of heightened awareness and sympathy.

Second Place
Blue Is Truth
Robin Storey Dunn — Austin, Texas

Leave Home

The first time a girl came in my mouth, bucking and loud, I took it as a sign. I felt like I could fly. Pussy was rocket fuel.

By the time I asked I'd already made up my mind.

"What if I run away from home?"

The girl was older, responsible, headed back to Austin and college. I was sixteen, punk, half-feral.

She tried to warn me off.

"You could be throwing your life away."

I thought that sounded perfect. We were both right.

She was in Lubbock to see where Buddy Holly came from. That plus Prairie Dog Town took twenty minutes.

We walked block after block of wide, still streets.

She smiled and said, "It's like a ghost town."

She didn't have to live there.

We fucked for lack of anything better to do. After a few days, when she went back to Austin, I had nowhere to go.

From the time I knew what it meant to run away I knew I would. The girl on billboards for the Runaway Hotline called to me like a used car salesman. Meant to discourage me, she stands in the rain, holding a sign that says ANYWHERE. The sight of her gave me hope.

When I was nine, I imagined I'd take off from the coast, Corpus Christi or Padre Island, if we went for a family vacation. If I walked east along the shore, I'd eventually reach New York City. It wouldn't be fast or easy—the Florida panhandle looked like a bitch—but if I stuck to my plan I wouldn't get lost. I'd keep a low profile and steal what I needed as I went.

The first time I ran away I was twelve. Too young. Lubbock was too small, too flat and empty for me to hide. Dubiously gendered, marred by freckles, topped with bright orange hair, I was a walking signal flare. Still, it took three days for the cops to spot me in an alley, chase me down, and drag me back.

Now, at sixteen, I was old enough, more than. It would be different this time, the decision birthed in a moment of joy. I felt full of confidence, bathed in happiness, like a shot of just the right antidepressants.

For some, antidepressants increase the risk of suicide. You get just enough of a bump, just enough energy, to follow through with your plan.

I didn't have a plan. I had no thought beyond go. I was in a borrowed room, in a borrowed bed, my face wet as a newborn.

The next time I tasted pussy I was forty years old. That's how long it took me to get home.

Water Babies

Growing up, kids always asked, "Where do you go to church?" but we didn't go to church. It was the first question after they asked your name. Kids of four and five would ask and I'd stumble, lacking the vocabulary needed to form a lie.

"Christian...First..."

I'd trail off and get confused looks in return.

At daycare, a gang of kids gathered around a half-buried can. One end was exposed, the other baked into the ground. When no one could pry it loose, a boy explained.

"Satan has aholt to it. Satan has aholt to the other end so we can't get it out."

Satan was there, inches away, malevolent, red, his fingers bony, his grip everlasting. I never believed in Santa Claus but I did believe this.

People talked more about the devil than about God.

I picked up what I could. God was an old man, distant in time and space. He had advocates but was rarely seen or heard. Satan was close, under our feet. He wasn't afraid to show himself, and if he caught you, chances are you'd never get away.

Kids at daycare avoided me, turning away unless they noticed me for the wrong reason, something I said or did. Then they pointed and laughed.

"You're stupid."

"You're gross."

"We don't like you."

"Nobody likes you," one boy explained, but I already knew.

Attention was never good. I tried to keep quiet and stay still but failed. I blurted out what came to mind excitedly, too loudly and at the wrong times. Something only I found funny or the answer to a question no one asked. The kids would turn to look and laugh or frown. Someone would say, "That's stupid."

Some animals run when they see a predator. I froze, hoping to vanish, chameleon-like, but my body always betrayed me. Against my will, my face prickled with heat and turned deep red, signaling alarm. Nothing like a chameleon.

One boy fared worse. The first time I noticed him he was backed against a wall, facing a crowd.

"Look at him."

"He's wearing makeup."

"He looks like a girl."

"A girl."

"Look at him."

"Why?"

"Like a girl."

Someone squealed. The boy was wearing blue eye shadow, plain to see from across the room. I stood behind the crowd, watching, and wondered how he got past his parents like that. He didn't answer but only stared, chin tucked, until the old woman who looked after us broke it up and scattered the crowd.

I saw him a second time, wearing nail polish. He was in the same spot, against the same wall, near the piano in the front room. The crowd seemed bigger this time, louder. I didn't see him again after that.

At home, I played in an empty field with a girl my age. A small tree was our only diversion. Everywhere we looked, the earth was bare, the sky immense and vacant. Nothing stood between us and the horizon, where everything fell off. Anyone could believe the world was flat.

"My mommy's better than your mommy, my mommy's better than your mommy, my mommy's better than your mommy," the girl chanted, walking circles around the tree, anchored as her hand slipped over its narrow trunk.

I watched, waiting my turn.

"My mommy's better than your mommy, my mommy's better than your mommy," I said, not really trying as my hand scraped against the bark. Putting my hand where hers had been didn't put me in her place. She'd picked a game we both knew I couldn't win.

I was safest in my room, alone, listening to records on my portable Fisher-Price turntable. Danny Kaye, Hans Christian Andersen, and *The Little Match Girl* kept me company. Listening to stories, I forgot my problems. I disappeared, surfacing elsewhere.

My favorite record was *The Water Babies*. It's Oliver Twist through the looking glass, a street urchin's adventures in Wonderland. We follow Tom, a young chimney sweep. He never bathes or goes to school. All he knows of church are the bells that ring. His master insults, beats, and starves him. Tom's best days are when he gets to have the dregs of his master's cup. When Tom's drunk he's the happiest boy around.

Eventually an angry mob chases Tom out of town. By the time he stops to rest he's practically sleepwalking. Thirsty and hot, he stumbles towards a stream, tumbles in, and disappears beneath the water, where he quickly falls asleep, "the quietest, sunniest, coziest sleep that ever he had in his life."

I met the water babies once, like Tom. Daydreaming, under a tree, I fell into a trance, an altered state. I found myself at the bottom of the sea with water babies all around. How welcoming they were, how kind. In their presence, I felt happy, peaceful.

Blood

My parents were immigrants—Mom from Germany, Dad from Trinidad. Everyone said it was an odd combination.

Mom was born in a bomb shelter in Germany at the end of the war. When Oma, my grandmother, went down to the bunker at the sound of air raid sirens, Germans controlled their city. Days later, when Oma resurfaced with her firstborn child, American soldiers filled the streets.

"They smelled so good," Oma said. "They had soap."

Three weeks later, Hitler shot himself in the head. When Opa heard Hitler was dead, he buried his uniform in a pile of pig shit and started walking home.

Seven years later, Mom didn't want to leave. In a photo taken at port in Amsterdam, Opa looks confident, Oma is smiling, but Mom's face is unsettled.

When it was time to decide where they'd live, Opa chose Lubbock, Texas over other cities because he liked cowboys and it sounded romantic. He imagined a broad river like the Rio Grande. They traveled by train. South of Amarillo they saw a large orange cloud sitting on the horizon. Opa asked if anyone knew what it was.

"Dust," someone said. "That's Lubbock."

The first thing they noticed was how ugly the place was. Dry, mostly dirt, not a tree in sight. They told themselves they'd leave as soon as they could but stayed, they later said, because the people were so friendly.

Dad came from Trinidad for college and stayed because his allergies went away in the dry climate. Trinidad was overrun with flowering vines and fruit-bearing trees, an abundance of pollen. In Lubbock that wasn't a problem.

We visited once or twice, and I loved Trinidad — the ocean, lizards, chickens, and goats, delicious roti and channa — but Dad said he hated it there. When I asked what it was he hated about Trinidad, he said, "Everything."

Mom called Dad's family "the last of the colonialists," always with a laugh, but I didn't know what that meant. They'd arrived with the British in 1797 and stayed to run a plantation.

Opa was a Nazi; Oma was one, too. They denied it, saying they never joined the party, but I heard the pride in Opa's voice when he mentioned Germans marching across Europe like supermen.

Oma waxed nostalgic now and then when she talked about Hitler.

"Those eyes," she'd say. "The way he spoke, he could get people to do anything."

Oma complained that no one ever talked about the good Germans. Mom agreed and said she'd write a book about it someday.

"Hitler was right on the race issue," Opa said, more than once, usually over family dinners. He meant black people, not Jews; some of their best friends were Jewish.

Mom agreed. She taught art at the black high school.

She'd say, "I know, I work with them."

She'd say, "I hate black people."

Home felt German, or at least not American. We ate *bratkartoffein* and smelly cheese, subscribed to *Stern* and *Der Spiegel*, played *Mensch Argere Dich Nicht*, and listened to opera. I spent hours with Mom's old copies of *Struwwelpeter* and *Max und Moritz*, German children's books. It didn't matter that I couldn't read the words. Color illustrations of death and dismemberment were easy to follow. Blood gushed from severed limbs and smoke wafted from the ashes of disobedient children. Bad children were baked, boiled, ground to powder, extruded as pellets, and fed to geese. When Mom threatened to ground me I thought she meant to bury me neck deep in the backyard.

Our house was full of books. I pulled books about the war down from shelves and studied the photos: headshots of criminals, mountains of skulls, and living skeletons only distinguished from the dead by their eyes. A copy of *Mein Kampf* sat on a top shelf, a gift from the state for Oma and Opa on their wedding day. It was signed by Goebbels, not Hitler; Opa worked for the propaganda ministry as a war reporter.

A line ran between those books, my family, and me. Guilt accompanied us but no one mentioned it, as if unsaid was undone.

They rejected the guilt. I pocketed it like a coin, something I could keep.

They wanted me to learn the language but I refused, only learning fragments:

Scheiße

Ich bin ein Hund

Ich liebe dich nicht

The first word means *shit*; the second phrase means *I'm a dog*; the third means *I love you not*. The last one loops in my head on repeat like a song. I can see Mom looking down at me, smiling and singing these words, but that could be a trick of the mind.

Oma called me *bienchen*, little bee.

School

I peaked academically in first grade. Never again would I see so many A's. I had an advantage because Mom taught me to read before I started school. It wasn't hard. Reading was the easy part.

My first-grade teacher, Miss Kate, was kind, but I still didn't make friends. The other kids didn't play with me or talk to me. If I tried to play or talk, they complained. More than once I found myself surrounded, backed in a corner with a crowd taunting me.

One day I came home and found Miss Kate with my parents. Through the porch window, I saw her sitting in a chair with her back to me. My parents sat on the sofa, listening. I was desperate to know what she was saying. I was embarrassed to think she was telling them about my problems at school, about what was wrong with me.

I ran and hid beside the house until she left. Earlier, while I was playing, I'd shit in the yard, and smeared shit on my clothes. I smelled like shit and didn't want Miss Kate to know.

I never asked why she was there and my parents never mentioned it.

Kids who kept their distance and made fun of me had reason. Normal eluded me; I couldn't unlock it. Once, on a crowded school bus, I saw Meg, a girl I knew, sitting up front. Her dad knew my dad; we'd spent time together at her house and mine. We'd eaten ChapStick together in my parents' bathroom.

I don't know why. I decided I'd crawl under the seats along the floor of the bus, from the back rows to the front. Kids called me names, complained, and made faces as I wormed my way through their dangling feet. Still, I persisted. When I popped up next to Meg I broke out in a smile.

The words "I love you" flew from my mouth as I lunged at her, my arms open wide for a hug. She'd never been unkind but she naturally recoiled. Her friends, normal girls, spoke for her.

"*Gross.*"

"*Gay.*"

"*You're gay.*"

I'd been called gay before, but it felt different this time, stickier, pointed, and made me uneasy in a new way.

I had no answer for them. I walked back to my seat.

Susan had freckles like me, but her hair was brown and straight. Her face was flat and round—she looked like Peppermint Patty, and was a tomboy, too. She didn't complain when she had to stand next to me in gym, and she let me talk to her. I got into the habit of following her outside after school. That's when I finally asked.

"Do you want to be friends? Maybe we could hang out?"

She was gentle but firm, and didn't hesitate.

"I don't think so."

Shame, chronic and acute, stuck deep. Shame was the thing I feared the most.

The trick I played to get by — the only trick I knew — was to tell myself it wasn't happening to me. Those things happened to another girl, some stupid girl, a girl I hated, too. I did my best to never look at her. When I had to, when she made a spectacle of herself, I told myself I was nothing like her. I told myself I was cool, tough, smart. I walked around in my head like I was somebody else, somebody strong.

This pretend life was precarious, the barest shelter. I was terrified someone could read my mind just by looking at me, and know what I was telling myself, that I was cool, tough, smart. If anyone found out that would be the biggest joke of all. I became my own best-kept secret, a secret I swore I'd never tell.

Third Place
A Daughter in Pieces
Nancy Hill — Presto, Pennsylvania

Omega

I answer on the third ring. The receiver cradles my ear like the shell of a conch, spawning a wave that sweeps me to my knees. Within its frosty wake, I perceive a vision of my ten-year-old self. A fearful message washes over me.

With heart pounding like the surf and eyes wide as the moon at its apex, I turn to my husband and say, "It's over."

Alpha

They said I nearly died as an infant. Wouldn't eat; rejected both formula and tea; cried incessantly; became dehydrated, scrawny, pale. There were dire predictions. The oft-repeated tale was dramatic: Aunt Julie, my mother's older and only sibling, demanded that Mother whisk me onto a plane to Kansas City, the ancestral home, where Julie had old Dr. Culp waiting. The venerable family doctor reportedly saved me with long needles, intravenous fluids, and mere moments to spare. It was said I could tolerate nothing but weak tea for a time.

Over the years, I became skeptical of this account. There were too many unanswered questions:

— Were there truly no competent pediatricians in my birth city of Washington, DC, in 1947?

— Were cross-country flights available, at a moment's notice, to carry out missions at life-saving speeds with affordable fares for average members of the general public?

— Was my father completely removed from this near-death drama starring his firstborn infant daughter?

— Who, in reality, feeds tea to a newborn?

— And those who know me well would ask, could I ever have been scrawny and pale?

As far as family lore goes, the story stood the test of time. In fact, years later, Aunt Julie claimed that old Dr. Culp had said not to let my mother anywhere near me. She did not elaborate about his rationale, but by the time Julie related that part to me, it made sense. By then, only too well, did I know of my mother's infinitesimal tolerance for trauma, something old Dr. Culp must have known all along. Further, I had learned from my own experience how unnerving a firstborn child can be, especially one as frightening and frustrating as I was. And, in my heart, I had long suspected that both Mother and I somehow failed our first, most essential bonding challenge. Furthermore, given eventual events, my father's absence in this drama was altogether plausible.

In truth, I never disclosed my skepticism toward this account of my earliest escapade. It fit with what later became my role with my mother...and was further confirmed by my father's relationships over time with both of us. Not to mention that, even now, I despise tea.

My mother's name was Violet—beautiful, sad, and shrinking. My father was Kermit, as in The Frog—he had been a frogman in the war. They named me Nancy, perhaps hoping that I, like Frank Sinatra's daughter, would become the embodiment of his song—my mother's favorite—"Nancy With the Laughing Face."

Our family triad spawned a tale of life, love, laughter, loss, survival, and lessons I learned along the way—some valued, others not so much. In retrospect, though, all the lessons were vital—how to look and listen, win and lose, seek and hide, connect and sever—to cope, to reinvent, to survive. And, over a lifetime, to attempt to understand and accept a sometimes funny, often frustrating, seriously fractured and, in the final analysis, nearly fatal family.

Inspiration

I like to say I come from a long line of writers...but when I do, I hope no one asks me, "How long?"

In truth, not so long.

My father was a writer, as was his father before him. My Grandfather Hill worked as a self-taught newspaperman in several small, backwoods towns in Kansas and Arkansas, jobs which led him to Kansas City, Missouri, and employment as a reporter with the *Kansas City Star*. In the late 1930s, Clarence Hill rose to the position of church column editor for the *Star*. Thus his son, Kermit, grew up in and around the newspaper business and developed an appetite for writing and journalism.

I don't know if the family writing gene dates back any further than Clarence, but I know that I owe some of my passion for writing to his son, Kermit, my father. That is, the man who was my father until I was ten—when he became my absent, ex-father. Like his father before him, he too became a newspaperman, editor, and writer. At age 79, Kermit wrote and self-published an autobiography called *Those Were the Days*. Shortly thereafter, he penned a fictional, semi-autobiographical novel about a news reporter entitled *Brad*. Although neither book, in my estimation, was of publication quality, they exist in print today...to be held, touched, scanned, scoured, accepted, rejected, shelved.

Perhaps because I myself did not appear as a character in my own father's life story, I am determined to prove something. If that father, such as he was, could publish two books, surely I can produce at least one. It is time. With clenched jaw, I say to my now-deceased father, this one—your daughter's memoir—is for you.

The author Toni Morrison is reported to have said, "If there is a book that you want to read, but it hasn't been written yet, you must be the one to write it." This statement rings in my ears as I find myself with a story to tell.

Humbly, I call myself a writer. One that has, from high school to college and through a career as an educator, met continuing demands for written product. Who has, over the years, excelled in writing, both personally and professionally. Who is regularly complimented on her authorings. Such kudos have charged my literary batteries.

In retirement, no longer required to write, I sought classes, joined writing groups, and began to pen my long-envisioned memoir. Still in my mind's eye are Emma Krumseik and Robert McGhee of the formidable English Department at Raytown High School; even now, I draw upon their confidence in my literary promise. And I think back to a year when, as a school principal myself, I imparted "words of wisdom" to a remarkable class of graduating sixth graders. I spoke of goals, asking each of those promising students, as they headed to junior high school, to identify a goal and be determined about its achievement. That day, for the first time in public, I announced my own goal—to write a book. I guaranteed my students that I would do it. That promise is almost thirty years old. It's time, dear students. This one's for you.

So how did my idea begin? Was it conceived unwittingly in a high school composition class with that demanding teacher, Miss Krumseik, who never let even one student off the hook...the feared honors teacher, referred to as the "battle-ax" by some of her less-than-literary charges? Who inspired not with warm validation but with iron-fisted determination? Who deigned to wring the best of thoughts from each of those students' seventeen-year-old brains? To see that such thoughts translated to errorless, if naïve, sentences and paragraphs?

Or did my story begin in another class, as I raptured at my literature teacher's daily recitations of famed passages despite the snickers of his less inspired young writers? As that lofty teacher-bard, Mr. McGhee, led us through centuries and decades of writings, which unwittingly inspired my own virginal pages?

Could the seeds of my memoir have been fertilized in college writing classes, even when the chief activity was watching the professor light and relight his pipe? Did the required readings in undergraduate literature classes provide fodder for my own tender syllables striving to germinate? Could all this take over fifty years?

I think yes. But it still may leave you to wonder why a completely ordinary person such as myself would presume to produce a memoir. I am not famous, nor a celebrity (whose memoirs, as you know, are currently all the rage). My story is no more remarkable than those of any other being who was once a child, who survived a family. Surely a memoir resides in the heart of every person who has lived for even a moment, a month, or a lifetime. Those stories, if put to writing, would be compelling, wise, witty, profound, fun...surely as memorable as mine.

But still I write...in vindication to my father, and to keep a promise to my former students.

There is yet another motivator—one which harks back to a hilarious evening long ago when I and my then-dearest friend, Emilie, were left to our own devices by our traveling husbands. A rapt listener, Emilie had heard—over the years—the tales of my tortured youth and fractured family. Amid peals of laughter or spasms of tears she, my personal writing cheerleader, demanded that I write a book. That evening, Emilie pulled out a notebook...and a second bottle of wine.

"It's time to get started." Her words slurred slightly. "I will interview you."

There followed a barrage of questions upon which I was only too happy to expound. Emilie took furious notes. Our session lasted into the wee hours. There was a lot of material. There was a lot of wine.

In the harsh light of the next day, Emilie and I were dismayed to find the copious notes of the compelling interview no more legible than the scratchings of a chicken. Page after frazzled page, not a word could be deciphered.

This debacle happened thirty years ago. Time passed. Both Emilie and I moved away. Sadly, we lost touch, for almost twenty years. Then, as life would have it, against a backdrop of serendipity and sunset, Emilie reappeared in my life. Ours was a surprising and unexpected encounter on a golden Florida evening among mutual friends. Without missing a beat, Emilie and I rekindled our friendship. I told her that my book was finally in progress. That, over the last year, I had penned almost half of the story she had found so compelling some thirty years ago.

"Oh, Nancy, really? You mean THE book...the one I said you *had* to write!"

Now two giddy septuagenarians, we relived the night of the famed, failed interview. Again we shared peals of laughter, wistful tears, wine.

Well, Emilie, it's time. The book is forthcoming. And, together with my other sources of inspiration, this one's for you.

So I say that a memoir begins at the moment one thinks there is a story to be told. The story can be long or short, complex or simple, ordinary or unique. It can grow from a tiny seed or an overwhelming landslide, or both. Given the right conditions—thought, care, love, support, luck—the seed will germinate. The writer will grow. The story will grow, perhaps into something that can be harvested, shared, consumed by others. And thus, that seed of a memoir, conceived so long ago, will be written.

Treat...or Trick?

It was Halloween, 1954. (Note: If you are tempted to dismiss this tale as preposterous, keep in mind that "back in the day," such a trick-or-treat scenario, although not commonplace, was indeed possible. This one happens to be quite true.) Picture it:

A darkening evening of Halloweening, uncharacteristically temperate for Rochester, New York. A sliver of a moon waxes above the fifteen or twenty identical, two-story red brick apartment buildings of the Strathmore Circle plan. Giddy trick-or-treaters gloat over the contents of their brown grocery-sack treat bags. Decked out in homemade costumes, princesses, ghosts, witches, and cowboys of all sizes rush home to enjoy the fruits of their labors.

The smallest of the marauders is unwilling to give up just yet. One last stop for a seven-year-old angel and her ghostly girlfriend...a building pretty far away from home, but still within the allowable boundaries. Porch lights flicker out like waning fireflies as the customary trick-or-treating time draws to a close. The girls, undeterred, knock with determination at one of the last lighted doorways. The door opens so quickly that they are unable to state their mission.

"Ah, girls—happy Halloween! Step right in. We have a very special treat for you tonight!" With that, each tentative youngster is presented with not candy or apples...but a tiny bundle of squirming gray fur.

A moment of silent shock is followed by unison shrieks: "Kittens!"

And then, a barrage of questions: "Do you have any pets? Do you live nearby? Will your parents approve?" More. All are answered in eager affirmatives and vigorous head nods from two jumpy second graders eyeing each other in collusion.

"Okay, then." The kittens are gingerly placed into the girls' gaping grocery bags. "But, just in case your parents say no, we will leave our light on for an hour. You can return your kitten by nine o'clock. After that, it will be yours. No returns after nine."

To say that we flew home would be an understatement. The buildings of Strathmore Circle blurred as our fleet little feet grazed the pavement from one corner to the next. After numerous blocks and only a few wrong turns, we reached our homes. I flew up the stairs and burst through the door, nearly overrunning my mother and father in the living room. Rapid heartbeats pounded in my ears.

"Guess what I got? But...we CAN take him back if we need to. But...but...it has to be before nine o'clock."

The words escaped without forethought or cunning. My blindsided father bounded from the couch.

"Him WHO?" He strode over and peered into the bag. "What the hell? A kitten!"

No doubt frightened by the fracas, the hissing little bundle leapt from the bag and skittered toward the kitchen in a frenzied flurry of gray fur.

"You absolutely WILL take him back! Who the hell gives a second grader a kitten in their Halloween bag? Find that cat right now!"

My frazzled mother shot into the small kitchen as the 9:00 p.m. deadline loomed. The kitten, however, was nowhere to be seen, hidden behind the free-standing stove—cozy, unreachable.

The 9:00 p.m. deadline passed once again—the next evening—before a tentative gray shadow crept out, enticed by tiny, furtive tidbits of kibble. In the meantime, despite ongoing interrogation, nothing surfaced regarding the apartment or building from which the preposterous Halloween treat had originated. Mum was the word throughout the neighborhood.

With undaunted hope, and with Mother as my conspirator, I conducted a relentless campaign.

"Can we please keep him? Please, please?"

Though rarely one to succumb to defeat, my father finally gave up. The furry gray critter was named Smokey. He had found a forever home at 20 Strathmore Circle. Though our family knew nothing about cats and had never entertained having one, even Kermit acknowledged that Smokey was a cutie.

* * *

A merry Christmas tree rose in the living room two months later. Fluffy, fat snowflakes descended outside, colorful lights bloomed within. Kermit's favorite Christmas accessory was unpacked. Rails snapped into place around the base of the tree. The little Lionel train began its holiday rounds to the delight of all, especially Smokey—who tirelessly batted the little cars off the tracks. Everyone took turns restraining the kitten to save the train.

With Smokey for entertainment, our little family snuggled together inside while a glistening white cloak blanketed the outside world. There were still a few cozy Christmases to be had in Rochester before Mother's holiday longings dictated that requisite Christmas pilgrimages to Kansas City would become the tradition.

Later that winter, I developed chicken pox and was quarantined in the midst of second-grade play preparations. Smokey was a loyal companion. But even that furry cuddler was unable to comfort me, the ailing Cinderella. I fretted. Would someone else be chosen for princess?

Providence intervened, just in time. Prince Charming too came down with chicken pox. He came to visit. Amid bouts of itching, we practiced our parts to perfection. The play was rescheduled. Mother applied the finishing touches, hundreds of tiny silver sequins, on my shimmering, white netted gown. Prince Charming and I recovered and the play was produced just after Valentine's Day. Smokey missed it, but he would soon star in a drama of his very own.

As is inevitable, spring came to Rochester. Smokey became a familiar prowler on the thawing grounds of Strathmore Circle. In those days, cats had both indoor and outdoor lives. I was sometimes awakened by screeching nighttime howls below my window. My parents concocted an explanation of some sort. By then, Smokey had grown into adulthood, sporting regal gray fur, with no pedestrian patches of white, brown, or black. His mesmerizing green eyes shone even brighter than those which reflected from my adoring face.

We children conducted springtime forays throughout the blooming neighborhood, but Smokey grew lazier and fatter. No one seemed to notice—too busy were we, cavorting in the fragrant spring air, absorbing precious rays of brief summer sun.

There came a day when Smokey could be found neither inside nor out. Mother and I searched high and low. He was too fat to hide in his protected perch behind the kitchen stove. He was not behind the couch—not under the bed—nor in the bedroom closets. Another closet in the back hallway was filled with winter things…coats, mittens, scarves, blankets…warm, soft items presaging the frosty days to come. In the back corner of this cozy alcove, we found Smokey—nestled in a warm blanket, encircled by three dewy, mewling kittens. Smokey had become a mother.

"Kittens!" Kermit exploded.

THE PENUMBRA POETRY AND
HAIKU COMPETITION

Poetry

Judge — Benjamin Dugger
Elizabethton, Tennessee
*"My congratulations to the poets for their fine work. I enjoyed reading
each of the poems and trust each poet will continue to produce
excellent writing."*

First Place
Lillian
Sharon Yencharis — Pacific Grove, California

Without money for Barbies,
we lived stories in the playground.
Interfaith Heights, home close by,
could not save us like the gods
to whom they thought we prayed,
nor could it teach us to rise above
ourselves, the people no one
wanted to be. In winter
we made snow angels,
flapping arms into white wings.
But our pop-up book motions
could not erase the dried ink
of our parents' mistakes
nor recolor this shame-bleached
landscape of memory.
No. We were a melting pot
of nopeople, lost, forgotten,
of color, uncolored,
broke and broken at 10.

But spring pulled us up from winter's ground,
our budding bodies still rooted in play,
and in summer we bloomed.
We scraped orange brick on stone,
made hopscotch boards
with the bones of real homes.
These numbers helped us
find our way out
starting with one.
We stumbled and fell,
sometimes forced to the ground
by grave boys raised
in violence. Our teardrops
scattered the sidewalk,
we mapped scars,
charted constellations of pain.
But some of us could
read those stars,
connect the dots,
count up from one.
We were the ones
who got away.

Second Place
The Gardener
Claire Scott — Oakland, California

The wormhole in my heart bewitches
with its smell of compost and deceit, and I fall again
dipping and diving through decades
until I land in the garden of my late twenties
and there he is
Strong, steady hands pruning the crabapple
clipping the green leaf laurel, moist with morning's dew
tenderly transplanting daylilies and hydrangeas
caressing them in dirt-creased palms
spreading mulch around tomatoes and lettuces
whistling while he massages it into the soft earth.
Faded Levis, scuffed steel toe boots
so unlike the Brooks Brothers suits of my life
so unlike the manicured nails
brown eyes shimmer in his sun-bronzed face
a tangle of damp hair under a Yankees cap
a grin that could launch a thousand ships
His hand lingers on mine while he shows
me how to separate the daffodils, the dahlias
how to store bulbs, waiting for spring's warmth
I ask him in for a cold beer
Circe to his Odysseus
he steps inside
A dry season for an old lady
living on the little that is left
sucking on memories

like the peppermints in my purse
hoping they will last awhile longer

Third Place
Shorelines
Robert Gibbs — Tallahassee, Florida

The morning sea salty with life
pounds the breast of the sand
and its shells of former lives,
then in resuscitating rhythm,
returns to pound again as if
to revive encrusted death
like some watery Ezekiel.
The thirsty sand welcomes
the living water like the
woman at Jacob's well,
drinking in its saving flow,
gratefully sharing her warmth
as the water retreats once more
religiously to its Source.
I walk along this living edge
not clear where sea and sand
divide, and make my way,
careful to touch them both
and let both touch me so
I may also feel unbound
yet connected to water and land.
The horizon, distant and distinct,
marks sky from sea as truth from falsehood.
Yet, no line divides the sea and sky, or
charts the coastline's claim to frame the land.
Approach these boundaries, they dissolve,

as one flows into the other, sea and shore,
water and sky, heaven and earth, life and death.

Haiku

Judge – Katya Sabaroff Taylor
Tallahassee, Florida

"Whether judging Haiku, other poetry, or short stories, the process is inevitably subjective. The Haiku I have chosen as winners might very well be different from another person's perspective. The key to remember: writing is its own reward, and the act of creation is not a contest!"

First Place
Yesterday
M. Shayne Bell — Rexburg, Idaho

yesterday sundown,
in that willow, a lark sang…
I know: I was there

Second Place (Tie)
Memories of elementary school
Renee Szostek — Scotts, Michigan

The principal kept
berating me for reading
better than the boys

Second Place (Tie)
Day on the Bay
M.R. Street — Tallahassee, Florida

Trolling motor hums
Kingfisher trills, rat-a-tat
Nary a nibble

2020 Winning Authors

We are happy to announce that this year, we have repeat winning submitters. Judy Klass and Christine Venzon both had winning entries in 2019, and Ms. Venzon was also a winner in the 2018 contest. Each year, we add to the list of contest notifications by including entrants from the previous several years. This adds to our outreach, and also includes emerging talents that we know are working on their craft and seeking recognition. We hope you will consider submitting your best works in the coming year. Congratulations to all the winning authors!

Ruth Andrews — Cassopolis, Michigan

Dark White is Ruth Andrews' first novel. She received the Golden Quill Award from the *South Bend Tribune* and has published essays, short stories, and poems in the *Christian Science Monitor*, *Sojourners*, *Inwood Indiana*, and other places. Andrews has an MA in Conflict Resolution and has worked as a mediator, facilitator, and sentencing consultant. She paints murals and works as an artist and writes from her Mennonite sensibility.

M. Shayne Bell — Rexburg, Idaho

M. Shayne Bell received a Creative Writing Fellowship from the National Endowment for the Arts (1991). His poem, "One Hundred Years of Russian Revolution," was a finalist for the Rhysling Award (1989). Bell's haiku have been published in *Modern Haiku*, *Frogpond: Journal of the Haiku Society of America*, *The Heron's Nest*, *The Wales Haiku Journal*, *Blithe Spirit: Journal of the British Haiku Society*, *Tinywords*, *Sunstone*, *Shot Glass Journal*, *star 82 review*, *O:JA&L*, *Haikuniverse*, and *Mainichi Japan* (where his haiku were listed among the best English-language haiku of both 2015 and 2017). Bell's poetry has also been included in multiple publications. Bell's book of poetry based on Greek mythology, *Blood Red Like the Setting Sun: Poetry of Hellas and Underworld*, will be published by Assure Press, Fall 2020.

Marina Brown — Tallahassee, Florida

Marina Brown is a journalist, poet, and novelist whose most recent book, *The Orphan of Pitigliano*, won the Royal Palm Literary Awards Gold Medal for Historical Fiction from the Florida Writers Association, and was named FWA's 2020 Published Book of the Year. Her two other novels, *Land Without Mirrors* and *Lisbeth*, have also won Gold Medals, both from the Tallahassee Writers Association and the Florida Writers Association.

Tom Cavanaugh — Edison, New Jersey

Tom Cavanaugh received his MFA in playwriting from the Actors Studio Drama School in 2000. Tom was a member of the 2019 National Playwrights Symposium at Cape May Stage Co. in New Jersey and currently is a writer member of We Make Movies Film Collective in Los Angeles, Bobby Moresco's Actors Gym in New York City and Los Angeles, P.A.G.E.S. in NYC, and Naked Angels Theater Company in NYC. For more info, go to www.TomCavanaughWriter.com.

Betty Cotter — Shannock, Rhode Island

Betty Cotter received an MFA in fiction writing from the Vermont College of Fine Arts. Her work has appeared in the *Hungry Chimera, Ocean State Review, Connotation Press*, and Bibliophilos, and she is a regular book reviewer for the *Providence Journal*. Her publications include the novels *Roberta's Woods* (Five Star, 2008) and *The Winters* (winner of the Rhode Island State Council on the Arts Fiction Fellowship, 2005).

Robin Storey Dunn — Austin, Texas

Raised by German immigrants, I grew up hearing "Hitler was right on the race issue" at the dinner table. At sixteen I was homeless, queer, punk, and feral when an all-Black spiritualist church rescued me. They said they were saints, and I believed them. For the next ten years I lived an ascetic, communal life. When it became impossible to stay, I had to find my way in a world where I hadn't yet learned to live. My work has appeared in *Gertrude*, *Perfect Sound Forever*, *Rue Scribe*, *Pidgeonholes*, and *The Windhover*, and won honorable mention in the 2020 *Tusculum Review* Nonfiction Contest.

Faith Eidse — Tallahassee, Florida

Born Canadian-Mennonite in Congo/Zaire, Faith Eidse survived revolution, disease, and abuse in a mission dorm. She won the FSU-wide Kingsbury Award for her MA thesis, *Deeper than African Soil*, and received her PhD in creative writing. She won Florida's oral history of 2007 for *Voices of the Apalachicola* (University Press of Florida, 2006) and has published several collections on growing up global. Eidse has spent 20 years as an adjunct professor at Florida State, Barry, and Keiser universities, and is coordinator of policies and training at the Florida Department of Health, Office of Minority Health and Health Equity. She serves as TWA's program committee co-chair.

Robert Gibbs — Tallahassee, Florida

Robert Gibbs is a retired United Methodist minister who has gone from writing sermons to writing poetry. He was awarded third place in the 2020 Southern Shakespeare Sonnet competition for his poem, "To Beauty," and his poem, "Lesser Light," is included in the Fall 2020 Volume of *Solum Literary Journal*. He lives with his wife, Brenda, in Tallahassee, Florida.

Lori Goshert — Tallahassee, Florida

Lori Laleh Goshert is an essayist, ghostwriter, and editor living in Tallahassee. She loves reading, animals, music, crochet, discussing social issues, and overanalyzing kids' shows. She gathers inspiration from her background in ethnomusicology, surrealist art, and experiences in other countries, including the Czech Republic, Spain, and Bosnia.

Yvonne Hazelton — Paris, France

Yvonne Hazelton is a Texan/Californian writer. Although she now lives in Paris, her fiction usually takes place in the Texas of her childhood, after the Civil Rights Act and the Feminine Mystique, but before seatbelts and Anita Hill. Long before Me Too. She has written her whole life—academic papers, newsletters, journal entries, blog posts—but only started writing fiction when she moved to Paris. She has tried her hand at flash fiction and short stories, then completed a master's in creative writing from the University of Kent's Paris School of Arts and Culture. Now she's up to novels. She also writes articles on women's issues, families, travel, and life in Paris. Find her work at her blog, Escaping the Empty Nest, or at Secrets of Paris, HIP Paris, and Inspirelle. When not writing, Yvonne enjoys reading, cooking, or *flaneuse*-ing (strolling) about Paris.

Nancy Hill — Presto, Pennsylvania

A writer for a lifetime, in 2020 Nancy Hill became an author, completing her first book, *A Daughter in Pieces*, a memoir which resided in her mind for over forty years. With credentials as a daughter, wife, mother, teacher, school principal, and grandmother, she is a member of Women Writing for Change, Cummings Library Write Club, and other literary groups. When not writing, she is thinking about writing, reading about writing, talking about writing, or doing all those things while golfing, swimming, or missing Bentley and wishing she could get another puppy.

Peter Johnson — Naples, Florida

Peter Johnson is a graduate of New York University where he studied English and philosophy. After graduation, he lived and worked in Africa and in South America, where he taught beekeeping to rural subsistence farmers. He has worked at a variety of nonprofits and now works for a homeless shelter in Naples, Florida. Peter is married and has three children.

Richard Key — Dothan, Alabama

Richard Key lives in Dothan, Alabama, with his long-term (long-suffering) wife, Laurie, and recently added cat, Velcro. He works as a surgical pathologist but has been writing short stories and essays for about 12 years.

Judy Klass — Nashville, Tennessee

Judy Klass is originally from New York/New Jersey, but she now lives in Nashville, Tennessee (she is also a songwriter), and she teaches at Vanderbilt University. Eight of her full-length plays have been produced. One, *Cell*, was nominated for an Edgar and is published by Samuel French/ Concord.

Kathleen Laufenberg — Tallahassee, Florida

Kathleen Laufenberg has worked as a teacher, reporter, editor and science writer. She lives in Tallahassee, Florida, and Asheville, North Carolina, with her spouse, Kent Spriggs, and their canine companions, Lucy and Theo.

Imago Mana — Pahoa, Hawaii

Imago Mana was born a dreamer on a Friday the 13th. Named Vanessa by her parents, she became Imago at the age of 50. That was the year she lost her job as a teacher, her home, and all her material treasures due to debilitating chronic migraines. With nothing left to lose, she retired on disability, left everything and everyone she'd known, and followed her life-long dream of living in Hawaii. She still lives in Hawaii, and in between migraines, she follows another of her many dreams, writing and sharing stories. Imago's biggest dream is to leave a legacy of tales that evoke laughter and tears, but most of all inspire those who read them to follow their dreams wherever they may lead.

Kenneth Robbins — Ruston, Louisiana

Kenneth Robbins is Professor Emeritus Liberal Arts, Louisiana Tech University and remains active in the classroom as an instructor within the Honors Program. He lives with his wife in Ruston, Louisiana.

Claire Scott — Oakland, California

Claire Scott is an award-winning poet who has received multiple Pushcart Prize nominations. Her work has been accepted by the *Atlanta Review, Bellevue Literary Review, New Ohio Review, Enizagam, Healing Muse,* and others. Claire is the author of *Waiting to be Called* and *Until I Couldn't* and co-author of *Unfolding in Light: A Sisters' Journey in Photography and Poetry.*

Lauren Strach — Yachats, Oregon

Lauren Strach is a nationally recognized fiber artist who has recently turned to writing. She lives on the central coast of Oregon in a small town very similar to the setting of this novel. *Wildwind* is her second novel.

M.R. Street — Tallahassee, Florida

M.R. Street is an award-winning author and publisher. She enjoys reading, writing, fishing, and watching wildlife at her Ochlockonee Bay, getaway. Reach her at turtlecovepress.com.

Renée Szostek — Scotts, Michigan

Renée Szostek learned to read when she was four years old and has been an avid reader ever since. She earned master's degrees from Northwestern University and Yale University. She enjoys experimenting with the meanings and sounds of words. Her interest in poetry is complemented by her musical and artistic talents and an interest in nearly every field of science and mathematics.

Laura Thompson — Nashville, Tennessee

Laura Thompson lives in Nashville with her husband and three children. A Montgomery, AL, native, she majored in history at Yale, earned a JD from Vanderbilt, and spent five years in Japan teaching English and practicing IP law.

Christine Venzon — Peoria, Illinois

Christine Venzon is a freelance writer and former textbook contributor whose work has appeared in general interest and Christian magazines. She contributes to the food encyclopedia *Entertaining: From Ancient Rome to the Super Bowl*. Her children's fiction has won awards from *Highlights for Children* magazine. She was runner-up in the *Saturday Evening Post's* Great American Fiction Contest in 2014 and 2017. She lives and writes in her hometown of Peoria, Illinois.

Sharon Yencharis — Pacific Grove, California

Sharon Yencharis is a technologist, artist, and writer, most recently having worked as Director of IT at the deYoung and Legion of Honor Museums in San Francisco. Her most recent book, written and illustrated in collaboration with her fiancé, Astronaut Dan Bursch, is *Up to the Moon,* the first in a series of four children's books. Yencharis also has a non-fiction book-in-progress with a mathematical formula for happiness called *Break the Alphabet: The Mathematics of Happiness and the Grammar of Change.*

2020 Judges

We thank our team of judges for their time, ability, and most importantly, their selections. All the judges commented on the consistently high caliber of writing, and how difficult it was to whittle their choices down to the top three.

Paul Donnelly — Ten-Minute Plays

Donnelly's work has won the Source Theatre Co. National Ten-Minute Play Contest, the Larry Neal Writers Award for Drama, the Virginia Playwriting Prize, and twice has been nominated for a Helen Hayes Award. Donnelly's ten-minute play, *The New Client*, was published in *Best Ten-Minute Plays of 2019* (Smith & Kraus). Donnelly's latest full-length play, *Memorial Day*, was read in Kumu Kahua Theatre's Dark Nights series in Honolulu; it was named one of eight finalists out of 1,243 entries in the first Moss and Kitty Carlisle Hart New Play Initiative. Donnelly is a member of the Dramatists Guild, Klunch, New Play Exchange, Playwrights' Center, Tallahassee Writers Association, and Working Title Playwrights. He proudly serves as the Dramatists Guild Ambassador for the Florida Panhandle Region.

Benjamin Dugger — Poetry

Born and raised in Elizabethton, Tennessee, Dugger graduated from East Tennessee State University and enrolled in the Southern Baptist Theological Seminary where he earned a Master of Divinity degree. He was a Baptist minister for 22 years, during which time he earned a B.A. with Distinction in

English and Creative Writing from George Mason University. He has taken post-graduate studies from several institutions including the University of Maryland, Wesley Theological Seminary in Washington, D.C., and the School of Scottish Studies, University of Edinburgh, Scotland.

Cheryl Jennings — Nonfiction/Creative Nonfiction

Dr. Cheryl Jennings is founder and CEO of SokheChapke Publishing, Inc. (est. 2007). An accomplished author, she has been published by Houghton-Mifflin Publishing, South-Western College Publishing, The Senior Economist, and others. Before becoming a full-time publisher, she spent 31 years as a teacher, professor, and university administrator.  During those years, she participated in numerous national conferences, was invited to Hungary, Croatia, and Slovakia as a consultant on economics and education, and consulted with non-governmental organizations (NGOs) in Jamaica, Trinidad, St. Lucia, and the Bahamas on health disparities, education, and entrepreneurship. She belongs to several publisher's organizations, including the Florida Authors and Publishers Association. She earned a PhD with highest honors from Florida State University. For decades she has been an active community servant, helping others in need. Throughout her life, she has enjoyed reading and writing and strongly believes *in the beauty and power of words.*

Ginger Marks — Adult Novel Excerpt

Born in Lansing, Michigan, Ginger Marks moved to the Tampa Bay Area of Florida in 1978. She began her career as a business owner in partnership with the medical profession. She founded Graph Inc., which eventually became DocUmeant Designs, which is listed on Design Firms.org and is a top-tier design firm out of over 20,000 design firms in the US. Her love for writing and design has been the catalyst for her successful career in the publishing area. Coming from a family of published authors and speakers, it was no surprise when she, herself, embarked on the writing journey. Ginger enjoys sharing from her vast expertise as a published author and business owner and giving back to her community, including as the Design VP with Florida Authors and Publishers Association since 2013. She invites you to register to receive her monthly e-zine, Words of Wisdom, which can be found at DocUmeantPublishing.com.

Joyce Sweeney — Young Adult Novel Excerpt

Joyce Sweeney is the author of 14 novels for young adults and two chapbooks of poetry. Her first novel, *Center Line*, won the First Annual Delacorte Press Prize for an Outstanding Young Adult Novel. Many of her books appear on the American Library Associa-tion's Best Books List and Quick Picks for Reluctant Readers. Her novel *Shadow* won the Nevada

State Reading Award in 1997, and her novel *Players* was chosen by *Booklist* as a Top Ten Sports Book and by *Working Mother* magazine as a Top Ten for Tweens. Her novel, *Headlock* (Holt 2006), won a Silver Medal in the 2006 Florida Book Awards and was chosen by the American Library Association as a Quick Pick for Reluctant Readers. Joyce has also been a writing teacher and coach for 25 years. She believes that writers need emotional support as well as strong, craft-based teaching if they are to make the long, arduous, but very worthwhile journey to traditional publication. At this writing, 64 of Joyce's students have successfully made this journey and obtained traditional publishing contracts. In 2020, Joyce joined The Seymour Agency as an agent representing picture books and middle grade fiction and non-fiction. Joyce lives in Coral Springs with her husband, Jay, and caffeine-addicted cat, Nitro.

Katya Sabaroff Taylor — Haiku
Katya Sabaroff Taylor, author of *My Haiku Life,* has taught Haiku poetry and Lifestories classes in the Tallahassee area since the early '90s. She believes we all have a poet/writer within us and enjoys the inspiration that comes from writing with others. Although she has been writing Haiku for 50 years, she says she "yet is always a beginner." She enjoys exploring and sharing this "essence" poem with others.

Sheree Reneé Thomas — Short Story
Sheree Renée Thomas is an award-winning short story writer, poet, and editor. Her work is inspired by myth and folklore, natural science, good music, and the genius of the Mississippi Delta. . *Nine Bar Blues: Stories from an Ancient Future* (Third Man

Books, May 2020) is her fiction debut. She is also the author of two multigenre/ hybrid collections, *Sleeping Under the Tree of Life* (Aqueduct Press July 2016), longlisted for the 2016 Otherwise Award and honored with a *Publishers Weekly* Starred Review, and *Shotgun Lullabies* (Aqueduct January 2011). Her work is widely anthologized and appears in  numerous publications, including *The New York Times* and *The Big Book of Modern Fantasy*, edited by Ann and Jeff VanderMeer (Vintage Anchor, 2020). Her writing has been translated into Spanish, French, and Urdu. She edited the two-time World Fantasy Award-winning, black speculative fiction anthologies, *Dark Matter* (2000 and 2004), and she was recently honored as a 2020 World Fantasy Award Finalist in the Special Award/ Professional category for her contributions to the genre. She lives in her hometown, Memphis, Tennessee, near a mighty river and a pyramid. Visit www.shereereneethomas.com.

Anna Yeatts — Flash Fiction

 Anna Yeatts writes in that nebulous overlap between genre and literary works where offbeat, surreal stories are born. Her short stories appear in *Cicada, Daily Science Fiction, Mslexia, Drabblecast, PodCastle, Orson Scott Card's Intergalactic Medicine Show, Penumbra*, and other publications. Anna publishes *Flash Fiction Online*, a monthly magazine dedicated to extremely short stories. When not writing, Anna

wrangles two wonderful children, two matching cats, and a German Shepherd who doesn't believe in weekends. Follow her at patreon.com/FlashFictionOnline.

2020 Reading Committee

The Seven Hills Contest Committee owes a huge thank you to our first readers. Our dedicated cadre of readers contributed considerable volunteer time in reviewing each and every submission assigned to them to ensure the highest quality writing was forwarded to the judges. A few were unable to participate due to technical issues, but we appreciate them nonetheless.

Mary Louise Bachman
Melanie Barton Bragg
Sue Bowditch
Katie Clark
Karen Cote
Charlotte Cummings
Sudduth Cummings
Jean Day
Lyla Ellzey
Jane Essig
Bob Gibbs
Judy Goodwin
Liz Jameson
Betty Lou Joanos
Saundra Kelley
Suzan Kurdak
Imago Mana
Jim Melton

Sally Mills
Marian Moore
Walter Moore
Bob Parker
Ed Radigan
Linda Radigan
Mary Jane Robbins
Johanna Rucker
Jerry Rumph
Brenda Scott
Carolyn Shackelford
Evelyn Shelley
Pat Stanford
Martha Stewart
Gary Stilwell
Sue Tabaka-Kritzeck
Judy Westbrook
Teri White

Readers may read in any category in which they are not entered. Please contact TWA if you would like to be a reader!

2021 Competition Open Call for Submissions

The 2021 Seven Hill Literary Contest and Penumbra Poetry & Haiku Contest will open for submissions on June 1, 2021 at 12:01AM Eastern Time. Deadline for Submissions is August 31, 2021. All submissions must follow the rules and instructions at **www.twaonline.org.** The rules, categories, and process for submission might undergo refinement prior to the contest opening. Please check the website when the contest opens for the finalized rules and other information.

The Seven Hills Review is a general circulation publication. NO NC-17 or X-rated materials will be accepted.

Judging is "blind"; therefore, any evidence of the author's identity in the primary submission will disqualify the submission.

1st, 2nd, and 3rd place submissions in each category will be published in the 2022 *Seven Hills Review*. First place in each category will receive a complimentary copy of the 2022 *Review.*

The following list of categories is not final and might be updated prior to the contest opening.

Seven Hills Literary Contest
Prizes: 1st Place: $150; 2nd Place: $50; 3rd Place: $25

10-Minute Plays: Submit a complete play that runs on stage in 10 minutes or less. No maximum word length; rather, the length is limited to 10 single-spaced pages.

Flash Fiction: Submit a complete story, 500-word maximum, any genre.

Short Story: Submit a complete short story, 3,000-word maximum, any genre.

Adult Novel Excerpt: Submit the first 3,000 words of an adult novel, any genre. Also provide a 150-word (or less) synopsis at the beginning of the document.

Young Adult Novel Excerpt: Submit the first 3,000 words of a young adult novel, any genre. Also provide a 150-word (or less) synopsis at the beginning of the document.

Personal Essay: Submit a complete nonfiction essay containing the author's argument or perspective in a maximum of 1,200 words. Any genre accepted (e.g., humorous, satirical, documentary) as long as it is factually true yet expressed in an elegant, literary style.

Nonfiction: Submit the first 3,000 words of a nonfiction work (minimum 1,200 words). Also provide a 150-word (or less) synopsis at the beginning of the document. Any genre accepted (e.g., memoir, travel, nature, news journalism, biography, creative non-fiction stories) as long as it is factually true yet expressed in an elegant, literary style.

Penumbra Poetry and Haiku Contest
Prizes:
Poetry: 1st Place: $100; 2nd Place: $50; 3rd Place: $25
Haiku: 1st Place: $60; 2nd Place: $30; 3rd Place $20

Poetry: Up to 50 lines, any style or subject; line length may be edited to fit final publication format; each entry must consist of only one poem (regardless of length).

Haiku: 3-line haiku, must conform to strict syllable count, may submit up to three haiku with one entry fee.

Previous issues of the *Seven Hills Review* are available at Amazon.com and through Tallahassee Writers Association.

Made in the USA
Columbia, SC
27 February 2021